WHEAT IN THE WINEPRESS

BOB HEXT

malcolm down

PUBLISHING

ISBN-13: 978-1-912863-21-1

To Anne and our children:
Shelley, Elizabeth and Ionë

In memory of Barry Cocker 1944–2017

CONTENTS

CONTENTS

INTRODUCTION AND ACKNOWLEDGEMENTS

Two windows

This book is about winning battles, just as Gideon won his. The story of Gideon is tucked away in the book of Judges, yet it is referenced in the psalms (Psalm 83) and also in Isaiah 9 and 10; notably in Isaiah 9:2-7 which includes the most famous messianic prophecy of all: "For unto us a child is born..." To walk in the government of Jesus is to live in the victory that He purchased. The Day of Midian (v.4) is a model of the victory that is won through Jesus (v.6). The two go together. Our battles may (will) be personal, and we may (will) be involved, knowingly or not, in wider battles that rage over a church, a city, or even a nation; but we are called, like Timothy, to "fight the good fight of faith" (1 Tim. 6:12) – not to fight and lose, but to fight and win. The Greek word that Paul uses, *agōnizomai*, refers to someone who is contending for a prize. So if all scripture is God-breathed and useful for our instruction (2 Tim. 3:16), it must follow that there are lessons the Holy Spirit can teach us from the story of Gideon on how to be victorious in our battles today. We can learn what it means for even the least among us to fight and win. We can learn what it is to be transformed from worrier to warrior. We learn that victory, and leadership, are not about strength, ability and numbers, but about faith, obedience and anointing. And we can certainly learn not to be deceived by appearances.

I'm looking out of my window at the moment and see a uniform grey sky, with one hundred per cent cloud cover. The clouds aren't the sky; they cover it. If the clouds weren't there I would see clear shining blue. I think one of the biggest lies that the deceiver spins to the Church today is that the grey sky is all we can expect, and that any moments when there is a break in the clouds and we even see a bit of sunshine are going to be exceptions. We get used to the same old grey, and the clouds become our sky. Like Gideon threshing his wheat in the winepress instead of the threshing floor, we function, but we aren't seeing God's best. Yet when we look through the window of scripture or read accounts of revival past and present, what we see is definitely a blue sky over the New Testament Church and some of its more recent incarnations. And so the question arises: "Why don't we see that in our own lives?"

There may well have been clouds that weren't recorded. The apostles may have laid hands on people who didn't recover. But even that thought can be an encouragement to us: if we press on we know that the sun will sometimes break through, because it did for them, and Jesus promised that it would for us. So if, like me, you see different views when you look through those two windows, and your heart tells you that they should have more in common; if, like me, you long for the action of the threshing floor but your experience seems to be hemmed in by the walls of the winepress, then I think you will find some encouragement in these pages to join me on a journey that leads to a different sky.

Some personal details and acknowledgements

In 2 Samuel 23:2-5, we find the following verses:

"The Spirit of the LORD spoke by me,
And His word was on my tongue.

The God of Israel said,
The Rock of Israel spoke to me:
'He who rules over men must be just,
Ruling in the fear of God.

And he shall be like the light of the morning when the sun rises,
A morning without clouds,
Like the tender grass springing out of the earth,
By clear shining after rain.'

Although my house is not so with God,
Yet He has made with me an everlasting covenant,
Ordered in all things and secure.
For this is all my salvation and all my desire;
Will He not make it increase?"

As with David, my house is definitely "not so with God". Although I was saved and baptised in the Spirit in 1984, for most of my Christian life I have been more like the downpours of rain than the "clear shining", and rather than being a morning sunbeam I have cast heavy clouds over those closest to me by my failure to walk in some of the most rudimentary steps of life in the Spirit.

Although His word may have been on my tongue on occasion while I was at church, many words that definitely were not His have been on my tongue on far too many occasions as soon as I got home. But He has made with me an everlasting covenant, and in His love and faithfulness He has been gradually – especially in the last few years – been driving away those clouds. So much of what I have written here expresses principles I believe to be true and which I aspire to, rather than lessons I am passing on out of the accumulated wisdom of a godly life, because godly is one thing that most of my life hasn't been. But I do know that God is raising up an army in these days, and that if we don't learn to live and fight like warriors we will at best miss out on the exciting victories that God has prepared for us, and at worst be picked off by the enemy and left wounded and bleeding on the battlefield.

Now I come to the acknowledgements. First of all I have to thank Anne, my wife, for being there. Literally. A weaker woman would have cut and run many years ago, and found herself a husband who knew the meaning of Love; but she trusted God through all the bleak years and has shown me what it means to "lean on the Lord". We have three daughters and (at the time of writing) four grandchildren, and they have to be the greatest blessing in my life. They are sweet and beautiful and I wish I'd been a better Daddy when they were growing up.

Who else to thank? As "living stones" we are all shaped by the Lord working through the other living stones around us; but I think the people that I feel the deepest gratitude to are those

4

who helped us and stood by us in the early days. Without them by our sides I don't know how we would have ended up. This book would certainly never have been written. Barry Cocker, who sadly passed away in 2017, baptised us and pastored us through one storm after another. Barry, you must have despaired of us at times! You were a true Gideon. Peter Worsley, you gave me the wise counsel that set me on the road that eventually led to founding our business, which has been central to our lives for the last 25 years. I would never have lasted it out as a career teacher, and I've never thanked you, so I am now. Andy and Ceri Douglass: I don't know where you are now, or even if you are both still on this planet, but if you are I hope this reaches you: your house and friendship was always a haven in the downpours. Maurice and Sam, for letting us use your caravan and for putting the children's slide on the roof and a green pepper in the kettle, which we will never forget. Andrew and Carole, for demonstrating what it really means to live a life of faith. And finally I have to thank Ruth and Basil Wolseley, Anne's parents, for accepting the unruly no-hoper who dragged their daughter off to his lair and always showed me respect and love despite all my shortcomings. You will always be a model to me of truly godly people.

There are many others, of course – encouragers, helpers, leaders, ministers, friends, colleagues, family, and all those who have taken the time to read this manuscript and have offered suggestions and corrections – I won't inflict a list of any more names on the reader, but you know who you are. Thank you. Finally, a quick word about sources. I've been reading the Bible for over thirty-five years, so I know it fairly well; but nothing like as well as the many and varied scripture references might suggest. Many of them would not be there if it were not for the Blue Letter Bible: if you want to study the word, it's the best online resource that I know. I strongly recommend you check it out. My standout favourite printed edition of the Bible is the Spirit Filled Life Bible, published by Thomas Nelson; general editor Jack Hayford. Its notes and features are rich in wisdom and insight. And of course there's Google, where I think we see something of the fulfilment of Daniel's prophesied "increase in knowledge" (Daniel 12:4). So many times I knew a scripture without knowing chapter and verse (literally), but Google gave me the reference. And there, in the very writing of this preface, we see the urgency that I feel to share the message of this book: we're living in the fulfilment of end-time prophecy, and it's time to take the battle seriously.

THE DAY OF MIDIAN

Walking in the Footsteps of Gideon

The people who walked in darkness
Have seen a great light;
Those who dwelt in the land of the shadow of death,
Upon them a light has shined.
You have multiplied the nation
And increased its joy;
They rejoice before You
According to the joy of harvest,
As men rejoice when they divide the spoil.
For You have broken the yoke of his burden
And the staff of his shoulder,
The rod of his oppressor,
As in the day of Midian.

Isaiah 9:2-4

Chapter One
The Winepress and the Threshing Floor

Terrified by the work of the enemy, Gideon is in the wrong place, hiding in the winepress to thresh the wheat. In this place of fear and oppression, he has an encounter with God – who doesn't see him as he sees himself. What "Midianites" do we face today?

I t's harvest time. The wheat has been gathered in, and it's time to separate the grain from the chaff. Time for the threshing. The Old Testament threshing floor was often on a hilltop, open to the wind which would separate the dust and chaff from the grain. Because of the open position the view was usually good – but this meant it was often exposed to enemy eyes and therefore vulnerable to attack. A crucial place, therefore, in the life of the community. It was imbued with particular significance in the reign of David: when the Lord stayed His hand of judgement after David had disobediently and arrogantly taken a census of Israel, he bought the threshing floor off Ornan the Jebusite, built an altar there and sacrificed to the Lord to offer his thanks. On this same site his son Solomon would build the Temple a generation later (2 Chron. 3:1), while many years previously another sacrifice had been offered at the same site, and God had also stayed His hand: this threshing floor was on no lesser hillside than Mount Moriah, where Abraham had raised the sacrificial knife to his son Isaac.

So the threshing floor was central in Community life, and historically was the place where the Temple was established. It represented purification, sacrifice and separation, and so had critical importance in biblical iconography:

"His winnowing fan is in His hand, and He will thoroughly clean out His threshing floor, and gather the wheat into His barn; but the chaff He will burn with unquenchable fire." (Luke 3:17)

It is the place where the wind of the Spirit can blow away the chaff of fleshly human thinking and the dust of the world; a place of openness, vision and vulnerability. It's the place where Gideon should have been. Unfortunately, he wasn't there.

In the winepress

Gideon was in a hole. Literally. He was in the winepress, which in some ways was almost the opposite of the threshing floor. The winepress was usually hewn out of rock and connected by channels to lower vats where the trampled-out juice would collect and ferment. Where the threshing floor was open to the wind, the winepress was sheltered. Instead of being good, visibility was restricted. Gideon was in the winepress – but he wasn't treading grapes; he was threshing wheat. He was threshing wheat in the winepress to hide it from the Midianites: *Working in darkness*

> "Whenever the Israelites planted their crops, the Midianites, Amalekites and other eastern peoples invaded the country. They camped on the land and ruined the crops all the way to Gaza and did not spare a living thing for Israel, neither sheep nor cattle nor donkeys. They came up with their livestock and their tents like swarms of locusts. It was impossible to count them or their camels; they invaded the land to ravage it … Gideon was threshing wheat in a winepress to keep it from the Midianites."

(Judg. 6:3-5,11 NIV)

Picture Gideon: he is tossing the wheat and chaff into the air to winnow it, but because he is out of the wind, much of the chaff and dust is dropping back with the grain. The hollowed-out basin in which he is working has a central hole in the ground, where the wine would drain down into the lower vats from which it was tapped off. Debris from the threshing – chaff and grains – would be falling down into those vats where it would later contaminate the wine. In addition, any grain escaping there would be lost to the harvest – and each grain would be precious, as so much was already being ravaged and stolen by the Midianites. Hidden away in his hole, struggling to winnow wheat without the wind, fearful every moment of the voice of the enemy, Gideon was a man immersed in his fears, stuck in his ineffectiveness, and cut off from the people around him.

It was here where he met with the Lord. Sometimes, like He did with Elijah, God will say, "What are you doing here?" But not on this occasion.

"When the angel of the LORD appeared to Gideon, he said, 'The LORD is with you, mighty warrior.'" (Judg. 6:12 NIV)

words like these have the ability to change our lives!

How often are we where Gideon was? Closed off to the wind of the Holy Spirit; forever picking the same bits of rubbish out of our lives only to find them cropping up again days, weeks or months later; hidden from – and blind to – the needs of those around us because we are down in our hole; unable to see the big picture for our preoccupations. Fearfully we look for the nearest solution as we run from the thing which is pressing – and in doing so we ruin it for future use. Whether it's the man with the unpaid bill who borrows on a high-interest "payday loan" and just compounds his debt, the unhappy housewife running into her lover's arms, or the nation's chancellor funding feel-good election promises with borrowed billions . . . these are people running from the Midianites and jumping into the winepress.

Treading the grapes was, and is, a time of joy and celebration. Nobody wants to keep picking chaff out of the juice.

So what do we see as we stand here with Gideon?

It may just be the debris of a disordered life, left from rushed tasks badly done – not with love and care, "as unto the Lord" – always fearful that we won't have enough time to do them properly. Wheat in the winepress. It may be the debris of wasted hours – days, weeks, months – left barren and fruitless by excuses and self-justification as we see only our fears and not the person next to us. Wheat in the winepress. And more critically, we see the results of lives habitually lived in the enclave of those fears, in broken relationships, wounded hearts and lost potential.

The world is threshing in the winepress. Destroying rainforest ecosystems to plant cash crops, we're eating our lungs to fill our stomachs. Half the world's steel comes from a few hundred square miles where the air burns with sulphur and yellow dust coats the trees, while the world keeps building its bank over a cavern of debt, ruining the future to satisfy present need. Like the Midianites, the devil is out in force to rob, steal and destroy. And Jesus calls us back to the threshing floor, for that is where He is building His Temple.

Bible references:

2 Chronicles 3:1
Luke 3:17
Judges 6:3-5,11 NIV
Judges 6:12 NIV

Chapter Two
Face to Face

When eventually Gideon realised that he was in the presence of the Angel of the Lord, he fell on his face. Today we welcome the Holy Spirit into our gatherings, but often this is without a true revelation of who He is. Like Joshua we need to remove our sandals and know that we are on holy ground: we are encountering the Living God. AMEN !

G ideon stands consumed by his fears, but the Lord does not acknowledge them at this stage. This meeting is about identity and purpose. Gideon sees everything that limits him; God sees two things: the person He has made, and the relationship that He has with him. "The Lord is with you, you mighty man of valour!" Gideon is not an insignificant wimp; he is a mighty man of valour. And he is not alone; the Lord is with him. Here is the full conversation:

"And the Angel of the LORD appeared to him, and said to him, 'The LORD *is* with you, you mighty man of valour!' Gideon said to Him, 'O my lord, if the LORD is with us, why then has all this happened to us? And where *are* all His miracles which our fathers told us about, saying, "Did not the LORD bring us up from Egypt?" But now the LORD has forsaken us and delivered us into the hands of the Midianites.' Then the LORD turned to him and said, 'Go in this might of yours, and you shall save Israel from the hand of the Midianites. Have I not sent you?' So he said to Him, 'O my Lord, how can I save Israel? Indeed my clan *is* the weakest in Manasseh, and I *am* the least in my father's house.' And the LORD said to him, 'Surely I will be with you, and you shall defeat the Midianites as one man.'"

(Judg. 6:12-16)

God's rhetorical question to Gideon rings out to us from the walls of that winepress, through the books of the Bible, and across the generations: "Have I not sent you?"

Jesus came to "destroy the works of the evil one". He sees the devastation caused by the enemy, and He sends us "into all the world" to bring Kingdom Restoration in His name. We have a thousand reasons to put off the task, but, as Jesus said to Martha, only "one thing is needed". Surely He is with us.

 "Go therefore and make disciples of all the nations, baptising them in the name of the Father and of the Son and of the Holy Spirit, teaching them to observe all things that I have commanded you; and lo, I am with you always, even to the end of the age."

(Matt. 28:19-20)

We may have been Christians for thirty years; we may be newly saved, but the same charge is on us all: Go. Defeat the Midianites and make disciples.

We read the Scriptures. We may know them well; we may even preach from them. We pray, we prophesy, we worship. We know God is with us – we hear it every week. It may well be that we live loving, righteous lives; that our personal winepress is fairly free of wheat. And yet we don't "go" – we'd rather stay. Maybe we've tried to share the gospel or pray for the sick, and our efforts have been fruitless. So we say, "Well that didn't work. Obviously it's not my ministry. How can I save Israel? I'll just stick with putting out the chairs on Sunday morning."

So why do our churches and our ministries so often lack power?

When Gideon first met with the Angel of the Lord his response to God's call was sceptical, as we have seen. Even when the Angel of the Lord went on to say that the Midianites would be defeated "as one man" Gideon's scepticism hardly diminished, as Judges 6:17 shows:

> "Then he said to Him, 'If now I have found favour in Your sight, then show me a sign that it is You who talk with me.'"

reassurance & confirmation!

Jesus is very clear about people who ask for signs to prove the reality of God: on two separate occasions He says, "An evil and adulterous generation seeks after a sign, and no sign will be given to it except the sign of the prophet Jonah" (Matt. 12:39; Matt. 16:4). The wisdom of God knows that humanity will not respond to His Person by witnessing His acts; seeing what He does will not cause us to seek Him more. Yet here the Lord grants Gideon's request to go and prepare a sacrifice, telling him when he comes back to set it out on a rock and pour out the broth.

> "Then the Angel of the LORD put out the end of the staff that *was* in His hand, and touched the meat and the unleavened bread; and fire rose out of the rock and consumed the meat and the unleavened bread. And the Angel of the LORD departed out of his sight."
>
> (Judg. 6:21)

God granted Gideon's request because He knew – and knows today – that only a real encounter would dispel the doubt. What happens to Gideon's scepticism now?   *So True !*

> "Now Gideon perceived that He was the Angel of the Lord. So Gideon said, 'Alas, O Lord God! For I have seen the Angel of the Lord face to face.'" (v.22)

Now God had his attention. And in that moment of revelation He showed His nature: He revealed His grace.

✗ "Peace be with you! Do not fear. You shall not die." (v.23) *✗*

A man who had a similar encounter was Isaiah. When he saw the glory of the Lord in the temple he cried:

> "Woe to me! I am ruined! For I am a man of unclean lips, and I live among a people of unclean lips, and my eyes have seen the King, the LORD Almighty."

> (Isa. 6:5 NIV)

And again the response from Heaven was one of grace:

> "Then one of the seraphim flew to me with a live coal in his hand, which he had taken with tongs from the altar. With it he touched my mouth and said, 'See, this has touched your lips; your guilt is taken away and your sin atoned for.'"

> (Isa. 6:6-7 NIV)

Having been thus cleansed, Isaiah could respond to the call of God:

> "Then I heard the voice of the Lord saying, 'Whom shall I send? And who will go for us?' And I said, 'Here am I. Send me!'"
>
> (Isa. 6:8 NIV)

If we will see it, the template is here. God sends us to fight His battles, but first He draws us into a revelation of His majesty and His grace. The two are inseparable. We need to hear God tell us we're not going to die before we can be effective in mission. Our experience of the fear of God is our measure of the grace of God. We know He is a God of signs and wonders. We have heard the testimonies; we have read the books; we long to see the power of God move in our churches. We read the Scriptures, and we stand in faith. And we wait, and try to hide our disappointment and justify our lack of fruit by talk of "pruning", "Digging down before building up" and so on. But I believe God is waiting too. While we are waiting for signs and wonders, He is waiting for us to "perceive He is the Angel of the Lord"; to pursue the encounter with Him that will truly reveal the glory of His grace.

The Bible gives us another encounter that shapes a mission, in the story of Joshua.

> "And it came to pass, when Joshua was by Jericho, that he lifted his eyes and looked, and behold, a Man stood

opposite him with His sword drawn in His hand. And Joshua went to Him and said to Him, 'Are You for us or for our adversaries?' So He said, 'No, but as Commander of the army of the LORD I have now come.' And Joshua fell on his face to the earth and worshipped, and said to Him, 'What does my Lord say to His servant?' Then the Commander of the LORD's army said to Joshua, 'Take your sandal off your foot, for the place where you stand is holy.' And Joshua did so."

(Josh. 5:13-15)

Are we truly ready to remove our sandals, shed all our comfortable preconceptions, encounter the Living God on His holy ground, and do what He says to His servants?

The Angel of the Lord today

In looking at the encounters of the past, we can miss the one that God has prepared for His people today. In the figure of the Commander of the LORD's army; in the appearance of "the Angel of the Lord" – whether to Gideon or, for example, to Abraham – we recognise the person of Jesus. But where, in the age of the Church, do we see the person of Jesus? We know that He sits at the right hand of God, so we do know for a fact that He isn't going to turn up in our worship meeting in person. Christian basics – God is Trinity: Father, Son and Holy Spirit. Our Father is in Heaven: we know that from the Lord's Prayer. Jesus was in Heaven, then He came to Earth, then He went back to Heaven.

Which leaves the Holy Spirit. Jesus said:

> "I tell you the truth. It is to your advantage that I go away; for if I do not go away, the Helper will not come to you; but if I depart, I will send Him to you . . . when He, the Spirit of truth, has come, He will guide you into all truth; for He will not speak on His own *authority,* but whatever He hears He will speak; and He will tell you things to come. He will glorify Me, for He will take of what is Mine and declare *it* to you. All things that the Father has are Mine. Therefore I said that He will take of Mine and declare *it* to you."
>
> (John 16:7,13-15)

The Holy Spirit receives from Jesus what Jesus has received from the Father. Jesus is glorified in all the work of the Holy Spirit, because everything that the Holy Spirit does and says comes from Jesus, just as everything that Jesus says and does comes from the Father – "I do nothing on my own . . ."

There are songs which ask God to "Come down . . ." or we can pray in the same mode, beseeching God to "Step down from Heaven" or similar. But He has already come down, twice: in the person of Jesus, then in the person of the Holy Spirit. Jesus went back, but the Holy Spirit is still here. And all the time, He is revealing Jesus, as Jesus reveals the Father: "If you have seen me, you have seen the Father . . ." (John 14:9). There are no more encounters with the Angel of the Lord, because the Helper, the Holy Spirit is here. As Gideon encountered the Angel of the Lord, we need to encounter the Holy Spirit. Let us remove the phrase "Angel of the Lord" from the description of Gideon's encounter, and replace it with "the Holy Spirit":

"Now Gideon perceived that He was the Holy Spirit. So Gideon said, 'Alas, O Lord GOD! For I have seen the Holy Spirit face to face.'"

Do we "perceive" who the Holy Spirit is in our meetings and in our prayer times? Do we even expect to? Or does He remain some sort of Christmas tree in the corner of the church, with gifts for a few people but largely ignored by most? Paul's great prayer in Ephesians 3 can only be answered in our lives by revelation: "that Christ may dwell in your hearts through faith; that you, being rooted and grounded in love, may be able to comprehend with all the saints what *is* the width and length and depth and height – to know the love of Christ which passes knowledge; that you may be filled with all the fullness of God" (Eph. 3:17-19).

We cannot comprehend the greatness of God, present in our lives by the Holy Spirit dwelling in us, by our human thinking. Though He lives within us, we need to perceive that it is only by His grace that "we shall not die". The power of the love that comes to us from Calvary, that reaches through us to the broken and needy, comes from the being, who, should He so choose, merely has to think a full stop to our lives for our existence to end.

Yet such a thought is as far removed from the mind of God as the East is from the West. Why? Because that choice has already been made and executed at Calvary. God looked at all the sin of all the world, for all time, contorting the face and the body of His perfect and only begotten Son, and He put that full stop to sin and to the punishment of the law for ever. It was finished. And now, for those who believe, the only thoughts that flow towards us from the mind of God are, as Jeremiah 29:11 tells us, "of peace, and not for evil, to give [us] a future and a hope".

Jesus teaches us to "believe we have received" whatever we ask in prayer (Mark 11:24). John 1:16 (ESV) tells us that we have all received "from His fullness", "grace upon grace". Jesus asks the rich young ruler (Mark 10:18) why he calls Him "good", and says that "only God is good" (by implication – "you are actually telling me that I am God, which I am, but you just don't see it!"). True goodness does not exist outside of God. It is a characteristic of the fullness of God that Paul longs that we are filled with. This same fullness "we have received" as God pours His grace into our lives. This is the revelation that we need: because of the cross, all of the majesty and awesome power of God, in all His fullness, is channelled to us in His goodness. The fullness – "the depth and the height" – of His goodness is no less the magnitude of that power to destroy which caused Gideon and Isaiah to give a cry of despair when they realised that they had glimpsed the face of God. Through the cross it is ours, just to believe, and to receive, in all its fullness, Grace upon Grace.

Bible references

Judges 6:12-16
Matthew 28:19-20
Matthew 12:39
Matthew 16:4
Judges 6:22-23
Isaiah 6:5-8
Joshua 5:13-15
John 16:7,13-15
John 14:9
Ephesians 3:17-19
Jeremiah 29:11

Chapter Three
Gideon's Task; God's Agenda

Gideon just sees the threat of the Midianites; God sees the problem behind it: Israel's idolatry. Before facing the enemy, Gideon is tasked to face the anger of his father and his fellow-tribesmen and destroy the Baal at the centre of their community.

God calls us to root out any idols that might pollute our lives. Unless we do, we cannot expect victory in any spiritual warfare that we face.

EPH 6 :v12 For we do not wrestle with
Flesh & blood, but against principalities
against powers, against ⊕ rulers of
the darkness of this age, against spiri
tual hosts of wickedness in heavenly
places

W hen God calls us, it is for His purposes, not our own. Jesus Christ "was revealed to destroy the works of the evil one" in order that "the earth shall be *filled* with the knowledge of the *glory of the* LORD, as the waters cover the sea" (Hab. 2:14). There is no part of the sea that isn't water. In the same way there is no cubic centimetre of the Earth where the rule and the reign of God's Kingdom – the KNOWLEDGE of the glory of the Lord – shall not extend. The prophet Zechariah said prophetically, and emphatically, of the Messiah, "He shall build the Temple of the Lord, even He shall build the Temple of the Lord" (Zech. 6:12-13 kjv). When Jesus says (Matt. 16:18 niv), "I will build my church, and the gates of Hades will not overcome it," this is the vision that He is expressing: the Temple of God, built in His people, filled with the glory of the Lord, covering an Earth restored to the perfection for which "all of creation groans in childbirth" (Rom. 8:22). From the beginning, through Abraham, through Moses, through all the heroes of faith recorded in Hebrews 11, this is God's agenda. If the Angels in Heaven had departmental offices, Habakkuk 2:14 would probably be a motivational poster on their walls.

So when God calls Gideon to deliver the Israelites from their Midianite oppressors, it is not just so that they could live in peace. So often we are crying out to God to make our lives better; to sort things out for us. "Lord, I need a job/wife/ husband/house/ healing", whereas the Spirit of God is crying out to us, "What's happening to my Temple?" In His grace God desires that we should receive the answers to those prayers, but Jesus clearly gives us the setting and the context: "But seek first the kingdom of God and His righteousness, and all these things shall be added to you" (Matt. 6:33). God had already sent a prophet to the Israelites, saying, "I said to you, 'I am the LORD your God; do not worship the gods of the Amorites, in whose land you live.' But you have not listened to me" (Judg. 6:10 NIV). The Israelites were not seeking the Kingdom of God. God came to Gideon to put this right, and when His agenda was in place, the benefits would flow to His people again. The Israelite nation would not break down their idols, so God sought a representative who would.

Gideon was given his instructions, and they had nothing to do with raising an army to destroy the Midianites.

> "Take your father's young bull, the second bull of seven years old, and tear down the altar of Baal that your father has, and cut down the wooden image that *is* beside it; and build an altar to the LORD your God on top of this rock in the proper arrangement, and take the second bull and offer a burnt sacrifice with the wood of the image which you shall cut down."

(Judg. 6:25-26)

Gideon had to put God first. He knew he would be risking his life at the hands of the rest of the clan, and that he was risking the disapproval of his father. But, following his encounter with the Lord, he knew now whom he had to fear; and it was not the rest of his tribe, nor was it his father, and nor was it the Midianites.

Now that Gideon knew the fear of the Lord, he could not disobey the divine command. And through his obedience to the Lord, he had taken the first step in establishing his authority as a leader over the very men whose idols he had overthrown. He dealt with his idols before facing his fears.

We may not build altars to Baal today, but we are surrounded by idols. Many of us may be waiting on the Lord for a breakthrough in our daily battle with the "Midianites" that seem to over-run our lives and our land; while the Lord is waiting on us to do some breaking down of our own. For a biblical study of today's idols, see Timothy Keller's excellent book *Counterfeit Gods* (Hodder and Stoughton, 2010). Focusing on "the gods of love, money and power", Keller writes: "An idol is something that we look to for things that only God can give." In my own life, before and after conversion, I have bowed the knee to all three of these, and even now I can only say with Paul, "Not that I have already attained, or am already perfected; but I press on, that I may lay hold of that for which Christ Jesus has also laid hold of me" (Phil. 3:12).

The idol of relationships

My own conversion dates from a moment when I recognised that there is only one God of Love, and that this God is not the one that the world offers. I remember a conversation with a teaching colleague not long after I had become a Christian, when I was sharing my faith in this God whom I had recently met. We'll call her Eleanor. She told me that she believed in Relationships. This was her god. She believed that mankind's highest fulfilment could be found in exploring and committing to relationships with a sexual partner (marriage was an option, but only an option).

Before salvation, I would definitely say (along with many other people like Eleanor) that this was my god also. Without a relationship I felt lost and incomplete. I married my first serious girlfriend at the age of 21; left her for someone else four years later, and by the time I met Anne I had a string of failed relationships behind me. I was 30 when we got married, and our marriage was in trouble right from the start. My idol did not deliver. I expected my idol to deliver happiness: I did not realise that it was I that needed to be delivered.

We very soon had our first child, and soon after that it seemed like there was no hope for our marriage. Anne's parents were Christians and one Sunday they invited me to church. It was a pretty little chapel in the grounds of a Silesian school. I went – not because I wanted to meet with God, but because I knew the beautiful surroundings and thought that I would find some peace there. I had also met the priest, who had seemed to me to be a man full of light. The parishioners would joke that this priest only had one sermon: "The God of Love and the Love of God". He duly preached it. We were standing to pray. I was thinking about our marriage going wrong, and the thoughts in my head were something like this: "Well, there are plenty of fish in the sea, if we split up I'll find somebody else, and I can see Shelley [our daughter] at weekends . . ."

Suddenly I saw all my past relationships, and the current one, line up like a row of standing dominoes, and all fall over. I realised that they all had one thing in common: me. I realised that any future relationships would go the same way. The thought that came into my head then was "I can't pull myself up by my own bootstraps", and for the first time I faced the possibility of a life spent without love. I did not think that I could live without being loved, and at the same time I realised that this is exactly what was going to happen.

So I said to Jesus: "If what he says is true, and You love me like he says You do, and if no woman is ever going to love me, then I'll have to have Your love. Because I can't live without being loved."

I was standing with my eyes closed. What I felt was almost physical: it was a comforting arm round my shoulders, and a filling, like I had never known, from head to toe, with light and warmth. And in my mind I heard a voice saying, "I will always love you. I will never leave you nor forsake you."

That was over thirty-five years ago. There is much more to this story than belongs here, and it is still being written. Jesus, the God of Love, revealed Himself to me, and although I turned to Him then it was many years before I finally broke down the idol. Until then it may have been hidden away, but it was definitely intact. And for many years our marriage, though it survived, was very weak. "Midianites" were everywhere. At the centre of my conversion experience was a revelation of the supremacy of Christ's love over human love: when we put Him first in our relationships, His love will reach through us to touch our spouse and meet their needs, and He will work reciprocally through them to meet our own. This is the dynamic of *agape* which flows from the cross. But the hidden mantra of the relationship idol is "how can we make our relationship work for me?" Unless we break this down our motivations remain ultimately selfish: breakdown is inevitable, Midianites run rife, and nobody is loved.

God's agenda has never changed: "Thou shalt have no other gods before Me" (Exod. 20:3 KJV). He sent the Israelites into the Promised Land with one task: they were to rid the land of the idolatry of the Canaanites. Instead of doing so, they allowed themselves ultimately to be corrupted. In consequence, they were banished.

In his letter to the Romans, the apostle Paul is very clear about the consequences of idolatry:

"Because, although they knew God, they did not glorify *Him* as God, nor were thankful, but became futile in their thoughts, and their foolish hearts were darkened. Professing to be wise, they became fools, and changed the glory of the incorruptible God into an image made like corruptible man – and birds and four-footed animals and creeping things. Therefore God also gave them up to uncleanness, in the lusts of their hearts, to dishonour their bodies among themselves, who exchanged the truth of God for the lie, and worshipped and served the creature rather than the Creator, who is blessed forever. Amen."

(Rom. 1:21-25)

When idols come before God, sin and immorality follow, relationships break down, and the structure of society crumbles. We see the consequence in the world today.

In the open "worship" of relationships, which gained public acceptance in the 1960s, and more recently in the rise of internet pornography, it could be said that the ancient gods of Baal and Ashtoreth are alive and well. But what other idols do we bow to in the developed world?

Getting an "A"

Tim Keller writes this:

> "More than other idols, personal success and achievement lead to a sense that we ourselves are god, that our security and value rest in our own wisdom, strength and performance ... One sign that you have made success an idol is the false sense of security it brings . . . [which] comes from deifying our achievement and expecting it to keep us safe from the troubles of life in a way that only God can."

The domination of this idol in modern society can be seen in the obsession of the education system with "Getting an A" – an excellent examination grade. A, conveniently, stands for Achievement. It also stands for Approval, Acceptance, Applause and Admiration – the list could go on. To what extent do our hearts crave these "A"s? So deeply embedded in human nature is this desire that it was behind one of the temptations that Satan presented to Jesus: "If you throw yourself down from the temple the angels will bear you up, and then everyone will sit up and take notice! Everyone will think you are amazing!"

We know that Jesus resisted that temptation in the wilderness, but He resisted it elsewhere as well:

> "Now when He was in Jerusalem at the Passover, during the feast, many believed in His name when they saw the signs which He did. But Jesus did not commit Himself to them, because He knew all *men,* and had no need that anyone should testify of man, for He knew what was in man."
>
> (John 2:23-25)

God knows our hearts. He knows our every thought, our every inclination. Yet, through the sacrifice of His Son, we are accepted into His heavenly kingdom. Through absolutely no achievement of our own, we become children of God just by accepting His grace. At the far opposite end of the spectrum of human achievement stands the cross of Christ:

> "He was *despised and* forsaken of *men, a man of sorrows* and acquainted with grief … Yet we ourselves esteemed Him stricken, smitten of God, and *afflicted.*"
>
> (Isa. 53:3-4 NASB)

"And being found in appearance as a man, He humbled Himself and became obedient to *the point of* death, even the death of the cross."

(Phil. 2:8)

Like the false gods of love and sex, the idol of the "A"s is an insidious, ungodly evil in our society. Again, I can testify to the shadow it can cast:

Anne and I run a company supplying literacy resources for people with dyslexia. Our most successful product is a reading aid that we designed called the Eye Level Reading Ruler. I had always taken the applause for the design. Anne had tried to tell me on many occasions that she had put much more into it than me, but I wouldn't listen: I remembered my moment of inspiration. It was not until 2013 – while I was reading Tim Keller's book, in fact – that I saw the truth. Yes, it was true that I had had a moment of inspiration – but actually this was God, not me. From then on, Anne took the idea and worked on it, researched it and perfected the design that we now have. It is her achievement, not mine. I had set up an idol – "my achievement" – which deceived me and damaged our relationship, in that I never really gave Anne credit for the game-changing contribution she had made to our business and thus to our lives. Since I put that right between us our lives have progressed more quickly in God than when that idol stood in the path.

Satan only comes to kill, steal and destroy. Idols can do nothing else. They keep us from the truth and block out the light.

The psalmist says, "All my springs are in You" (Ps. 87:7). We need to ask the Holy Spirit to help us to root out and destroy any idols, and to be committed like Gideon in breaking them down; so we can find the source of our love and acceptance in Christ. If we ask Him, He will most certainly do it. It is top of His agenda.

Bible references

Habakkuk 2:14
Zechariah 6:12-13
Romans 8:22
Matthew 6:33
Judges 6:10
Judges 6:25-26
Philippians 3:12
Romans 1:21-25
John 2:23-25
Isaiah 53:3-4
Philippians 2:8
Psalm 87:7

Chapter Four
Blowing the Trumpet

The Trumpet heralds God's presence and proclaims His victory. Whatever our battle, it is essential that we blow the trumpet before we engage with the enemy.

At this point Gideon could have said, "It gets worse before it gets better." Up till now the Israelites had been plagued by raiding parties of Midianites and Amalekites. Now "all the Midianites and Amalekites, the people of the East, gathered together; and they crossed over and encamped in the Valley of Jezreel" (Judg. 6:33).

He had accomplished God's primary purpose and torn down the altar to Baal. He had done it by night, for fear of the men of the city, and also for fear of his father's household; so it may have come as a surprise when Joash his father stood by his side as he faced his clan by the broken altar early in the morning. "Let Baal plead against him," he said, "since he has torn down his altar!", and he gave him the name Jerubaal, which means "let Baal contend".

Contend he did. Satan cherishes his idols. He craves worship, he delights in anything that will keep men's eyes away from the truth, and he also loves to see division sown in families. Joash had tolerated the idolatry, and probably even paid for the idol to be erected; but now it was gone he had rediscovered his heart for God and he stood in unity with his son. Gideon had kicked the hornets' nest: now they were out to get him in earnest.

Paul tells us that we do not fight flesh and blood, but "spiritual hosts of wickedness in the heavenly places" (Eph. 6:12). Sometimes, when the Midianites in our lives come to steal or destroy, we forget where the battle rages, and in doing so we also forget where our victory lies. The escalation of the attack in the story of Gideon reminds us of the reality. The Midianite leaders neither knew nor cared that Baal's altar had been destroyed, but Satan did: he took it personally, and it was he who gathered them for an attempted final onslaught. Why else would "all . . . the people of the East" choose this moment to focus their attention on wiping out Israel? The real battle, then as now, was in the heavenlies.

In today's world the tribes may have different names, but spiritually nothing has changed. Luke 21 and Matthew 24 give parallel accounts of the Olivet discourse, when the disciples ask Jesus: "Tell us, when shall these things be? and what shall be the sign of thy coming, and of the end of the world?" (Matt. 24:3 KJV). If we put the details of both the gospel accounts together, we get prophecies of political and natural upheaval, persecution of the faithful along with the promise of salvation and the exhortation to endure, and specific reference to Jerusalem being surrounded by armies, along with the "Abomination of desolation" standing in the Holy Place. (Some prophetic ministries and "Jerusalem watchers" see these signs being fulfilled even now.)

The end-time prophecy of Jesus confirms the words of Daniel, spoken centuries earlier during the time of exile: "And forces shall be mustered by him, and they shall defile the sanctuary fortress; then they shall take away the daily *sacrifices,* and place *there* the abomination of desolation" (Dan. 11:31). The prophecy of the "little horn" in Daniel 8 appears to refer to the same time:

"Then I heard a holy one speaking; and *another* holy one said to that certain *one* who was speaking, 'How long *will* the vision *be, concerning* the daily *sacrifices* and the transgression of desolation, the giving of both the sanctuary and the host to be trampled underfoot?'" (v.31)

Daniel's prophecies and the Olivet discourse refer to the same time frame: a context where God's people are under great persecution and Jerusalem is on the brink of annihilation. What the enemy was seeking in Gideon's time appears to be finally in his grasp. It is just the conclusion that is not in his script: "He shall even rise against the Prince of princes; but he shall be broken without *human* means" (Dan. 8:25).

The sound of the trumpet

Here is Matthew's account of the last chapter of this age, when the power of the enemy is "broken without human means":

"Then the sign of the Son of Man will appear in heaven, and then all the tribes of the earth will mourn, and they will see the Son of Man coming on the clouds of heaven with power and great glory. And He will send His angels with a great sound of a trumpet, and they will gather together His elect from the four winds, from one end of heaven to the other."

(Matt. 24:30-31)

A trumpet sounded, and God's final victory, assured from the very beginning, was accomplished. This end-time scenario gives us a vivid picture of the nature of the spiritual warfare in which we are caught up: the battle is always over the Holy Place, and however the tide seems to turn, the ultimate victory is always with the Lord. In the time of Gideon, in end-time Jerusalem, and in our hearts today, the devil's desire is to usurp and trample underfoot the place of worship where God would have His throne. As Paul notes, we cannot engage in this battle with flesh and blood: when the enemy gathers his armies together, our response must be to blow the trumpet.

> "But the Spirit of the LORD came upon Gideon; then he blew the trumpet, and the Abiezrites gathered behind him."
>
> (Judg. 6:34)

Who blew the first trumpet?

The trumpet first appears at a seminal moment in the history of God's people. Three months out of Egypt, and the children of Israel are camped at the foot of Mount Sinai. God called Moses and announced the terms of the covenant. He said that all the earth belonged to Him, but if Israel kept His law they would be His special people, a Kingdom of priests, a holy nation, chosen out of all the tribes of the Earth to be blessed by Him and represent Him to humankind. The days that followed – when God the Father came in His glory to meet with Man, when Moses, Aaron and the seventy elders saw the God of Israel; when Moses went up into the cloud to receive the Law – have to be the most momentous episode in the history of the human race. At no other time, before or since, has Man stood on the threshold of the heavenly realm and gazed into glory:

> "Then it came to pass on the third day, in the morning, that there were thunderings and lightnings, and a thick cloud on the mountain; *and the sound of the trumpet was very loud,* so that all the people who *were* in the camp trembled. And Moses brought the people out of the camp to meet with God, and they stood at the foot of the mountain."

(Exod. 19:16-17)

The first reference to the trumpet in the Scriptures occurs four verses earlier: "When the trumpet sounds long, they shall come near the mountain" (v.13), and here we see its full prophetic significance: whether for blessing, as here, or for judgement, as in the seven trumpets of the book of Revelation, the sound of the trumpet in scripture heralds the meeting of God with Man. And, just like the seven final blasts, this first trumpet, sounded long and loud from within the cloud of God's glory, was not blown by any human breath.

✳ Breath of God ✳

Heavenly breath announcing the presence of God. Does this have a resonance? I think so. We know from many references in the Old and New Testaments that *Ruach*, or breath, represents the Holy Spirit, the Presence of God with man. In this light let us return to the events of the story of Gideon.

On God's instructions, Gideon broke the power of idolatry among the people who, not many generations previously, had stood before God at Sinai. Satan immediately amassed his Midianite and Amalekite armies, and Israel was threatened with annihilation. The next thing that happened was that "the Spirit of the LORD came upon Gideon; then he blew the trumpet" (Judg. 6:34).

So the first lesson of Gideon's trumpet is quite simple: if "the battle belongs to the Lord", we cannot fight it without His power. In modern times, the word "trumpet" suggests a brass musical instrument with three valves for producing notes, and we must remember that the "trumpet" sounded at Sinai and blown by Gideon was the *shofar*, or ram's horn. Probably the best-known of God's victories where the *shofar* features in the account is the fall of Jericho:

> "Then seven priests bearing seven trumpets of rams' horns before the ark of the LORD went on continually and blew with the trumpets. And the armed men went before them. But the rear guard came after the ark of the LORD, while *the priests* continued blowing the trumpets."

(Josh. 6:13)

The *shofar* sounded, the presence of God was with the army as the priests carried the Ark, the people shouted, and the walls collapsed. We don't know what the actual shout was, but it was a shout of victory. "And the seventh time it happened, when the priests blew the trumpets that Joshua said to the people: 'Shout, for the LORD has given you the city!'" (Josh. 6:16).

The word used for Shout, *ruwa* is a root word that can mean

1. a shout a war-cry or alarm of battle
2. to sound a signal for war or march
3. to shout in triumph (over enemies)
4. to shout in applause

The suggestion here is clearly the third one: God has given the victory; shout it out! The battle was the Lord's: it was He who had given the city. His presence was represented in the Ark, and it was heralded by the trumpets. As it was in that first angelic blast on Sinai, so it was at Jericho: the sounding of the trumpets heralded the presence of God.

Worship and idolatry

We find another battle scene in 2 Chronicles 13. Solomon's kingdom is divided. The idolatrous Jeroboam has led Israel against Judah, under King Abijah. Again, we see the spiritual forces of evil lined up against true worship, seeking to stamp it out. Abijah's army is half the size of Jeroboam's, but he knows the Lord is with him. He stands on a mountain and declares to the enemy that they are fighting a people who are in covenant with God (v.5), and who have not forsaken him (v.10); whereas they are fighting under a leader who is in rebellion and has no true authority (v.6), with priests who have no anointing (v.9). Because of their spiritual bank-ruptcy, they are powerless in their arrogance:

"'And now you think to withstand the kingdom of the LORD, which is in the hand of the sons of David; and you are a great multitude, and with you are the gold calves which Jeroboam made for you as gods . . . Now look, God Himself is with us as *our* head, and His priests with sounding trumpets to sound the alarm against you.' And when Judah looked around, to their surprise the battle line was at both front and rear; and they cried out to the LORD, and the priests sounded the trumpets. Then the men of Judah gave a shout; and as the men of Judah shouted, it happened that God struck Jeroboam and all Israel before Abijah and Judah."

(2 Chron. 13:8-15)

The word translated in v.13 as "sound the alarm" is the same word *ruwa* that is used for "shout" at the fall of Jericho in Joshua 6:16; it is the war-cry of the army of God, heralding the victorious presence of its King.

What happened when true worship faced idolatry? Firstly, Abijah stood on the mountain. He saw the battlefield from above. How often do we forget to climb the mountain and see our battles from above? This is our position in the Spirit. We are already raised with Jesus, and with Him we can look down on our battles from His perspective; the position of victory. We return to this topic in chapter eleven. We see more clearly from a higher place!

Next, Abijah spoke the truth. We know from Ephesians 6 that the word of God is "the sword of the Spirit", and the one offensive

50

weapon that we have been given in the battle against our adversary. Just as David declared to Goliath that he would not stand against the Lord, Abijah speaks out the same truth – the truth which is our inheritance, spoken of by Paul in that great passage in Romans 8: "If God is for us, who can be against us?"

The Spirit of God performs His word

The enemy doesn't listen, though. We know that he "walks about like a roaring lion, seeking whom he may devour" (1 Pet. 5:8). When we tell him the truth about our victory and his destiny, he doesn't scratch his head and say: "Do you know what, you're right", and leave us alone. Even after the third time Jesus Himself quoted scripture in the desert, the devil, we are told, only departed until he could find another opportune moment. No: the father of lies does not wilt in the face of the truth – he just does what Jeroboam did, and that's sneak round behind us to ambush us from the rear. When we speak the truth of scripture our wielding of the words alone does not defeat the enemy, as if we could pick them up and just use them to chop off the dragon's head. The word of God is the sword of the Spirit, and it's the Spirit who wields the sword, not us. The sword is in God's hands, not ours – or if it is in our hands, then God's hands are closed firmly round them!

When the army of Judah found that they were surrounded, "they cried out to the Lord, and the priests blew the trumpets": the presence of God came, and He struck down the enemy. God Himself makes the distinction between speaking the word and performing it:

"For I am the LORD. I speak, and the word which I speak will come to pass; it will no more be postponed; for in your days, O rebellious house, I will say the word and perform it, says the Lord GOD."

(Ezek. 12:25)

In 1947, Smith Wigglesworth prophesied:

"When the new church phase is on the wane, there will be evidenced in the churches something that has not been seen before: a coming together of those with an emphasis on the Word and those with an emphasis on the Spirit. When the Word and the Spirit come together, there will be the biggest movement of the Holy Spirit that the nation, and indeed the world, has ever seen. It will mark the beginning of a revival that will eclipse anything that has been witnessed within these shores, even the Wesleyan and the Welsh revivals of former years. The outpouring of God's Spirit will flow over from the UK to the mainland of Europe, and from there will begin a missionary move to the ends of the earth."

The word comes to pass because the Spirit of the Lord performs it. The sword strikes when the Spirit wields it. The gospel of Mark concludes: "And they went out and preached everywhere, the Lord working with *them* and confirming the word through the accompanying signs. Amen" (Mark 16:20).

Unless the trumpet heralds the presence of God, the battle is not won. We must not go into battle unless we know in our hearts – not in our heads – that God is with us to perform the victory that His word declares.

Bible references

Judges 6:33
Ephesians 6:12
Matthew 24:3
Matthew 24:30-31
Daniel 11:31
Daniel 8:25
Judges 6:34
Exodus 19:13-17
Joshua 6:13,16
2 Chronicles 13:8-15
Romans 8:31
1 Peter 5:8
Ezekiel 12:25
Mark 16:10

Chapter Five
The Horn of Anointing

Kingdom Authority is God-given and takes the form of servanthood, not domination. Men gathered to Gideon, as also to David, because the Spirit of the Lord was on him. In the Church true leadership lies with those on whom an anointing for ministry rests, and in whom we see the character of Jesus being formed.

"But the Spirit of the Lord came upon Gideon; then he blew the trumpet, and the Abiezrites gathered behind him" (Judg. 6:34). (Literally "Abiezer gathered behind him".)

We have seen how, prophetically, the trumpet (*shofar*) blast heralds the presence of God. The second aspect to consider is the relevance of the horn to leadership and authority.

The model of political authority we are given in the Bible is that of King David. Our King Jesus, in the human frame of reference, is "the son of David"; He is "of David's line". The kingdom of God among men began with a shepherd boy and a horn of oil. We read in 1 Samuel 16 that Samuel took a horn of oil and anointed David, the youngest and least significant of the sons of Jesse, to be the future King of Israel. As the blast of breath through the horn represents the presence of the Spirit of God, so the anointing oil here, poured out from the horn, represents His authority.

As authority itself is God-given, the sphere of that authority also is God-given. Although David was supernaturally gifted from the time of his anointing onward, the sphere in which he moved in the power of that anointing was limited to his work as a shepherd and the responsibility he had been given to protect the sheep from wild beasts. A time came later when, cloaked in the anointing of God rather than the armour of Saul, he came into the service of the King. Yet at no time does David presume upon his gifting to extend his sphere of authority. As we know from 1 Samuel 24:6, when Saul is seeking his life, he forbears from laying his hand on God's anointed king.

Even after the death of Saul, David makes no assumptions. Instead, he asks the Lord, "What now? Shall I go up to one of the cities of Judah?" The Lord tells him to go to Hebron, so he settles there with the men who had been following him up till then, along with their families. Eventually the men of Hebron come to David and crown him as King of Judah (2 Sam. 2:4). At this point Ishbosheth, the son of Saul, is reigning over the rest of Israel; only Judah had come to David.

Two years later Ishbosheth was assassinated. When his murderers brought David the news of the death of "the son of Saul, your enemy", their reward was execution, such was David's abhorrence of the idea that he should promote his own position. Finally, the authority that he had consistently refused to take upon himself was given to him.

> "Then all the tribes of Israel came to David at Hebron and spoke, saying, 'Indeed we *are* your bone and your flesh. Also, in time past, when Saul was king over us, you were the one who led Israel out and brought them in; and the Lord said to you, "You shall shepherd My people Israel, and be ruler over Israel."' Therefore all the elders of Israel came to the king at Hebron, and King David made a covenant with them at Hebron before the Lord. And they anointed David king over Israel."
>
> (2 Sam. 5:1-3)

David's leadership was recognised by the people: they gathered to him and made him their king, so fulfilling that stage of God's purpose for his life, and for theirs. When the Holy Spirit came upon Gideon and he blew the trumpet, the clan of Abiezer gathered to him. He was "the least in his clan", and he had just defied the custom of his day by breaking down the altar to Baal; but his anointing was recognised and his leadership established. Abiezer means in Hebrew "My father is Help". Gideon's leadership was marked from the outset by the fact that the Helper was behind him. When he sent out messengers to the rest of Israel to join him, his spiritual authority was already established.

The blackboard monitor

The desire for pre-eminence is deep-seated in the heart of men. Satan knew this well when he tempted Jesus with "all the kingdoms of this world". It rose up in James and John when they asked to be seated on thrones to the right and to the left of Jesus. History, in the Bible and through all of time, is littered with the corpses of rulers assassinated by the ones who sought their position. The career path of success in the corporate world can be fairly accurately measured in terms of how many people somebody is "over". We have team leaders, middle managers, senior managers, directors, all sitting on branches further and further up "the tree" with more and more people beneath them. Teams have captains and vice-captains, schools have prefects, gangs have their bosses, and so it goes on. Terry Pratchett satirises this tendency wonderfully in the Discworld novels when the title of "Blackboard Monitor" is conferred on the already much-decorated Commander Vimes. I remember as a small boy, in the far-off 1950s when we roamed freely through our village and the surrounding countryside, when a little group of us used to meet up for the day's adventures and someone would say, "I'm the leader!" Sometimes it was hotly contested, sometimes it wasn't; but it was always the childish cry of the human soul longing for recognition.

Jesus gives us the kingdom perspective, however:

> "But Jesus called them to *Himself* and said to them, 'You know that those who are considered rulers over the Gentiles lord it over them, and their great ones exercise authority over them. Yet it shall not be so among you; but whoever desires to become great among you shall be your servant. And whoever of you desires to be first shall be slave of all.'"

(Mark 10:42-44)

The human soul strives to "exercise authority" over others; everybody wants to be Blackboard Monitor. Sadly, the Church is not exempt, and a common temptation held out to even mature Christians succumb is the lure of ambition, the appeal of the badge of office, of being a "recognised ministry". I wrestled with that one myself for many years. Sometimes "I just want to serve" actually means "I just want to be *seen* to serve". But it's also important to note that Jesus doesn't rule out the desire to be "great", or even to be "first": what He tells us is that the route to that position is not to follow the world's path of "lording it" over others, but to be a servant. Authority is God-given; it is not to be taken. We must recognise also that Jesus is only pointing to the way to start out in that pursuit of leadership: the fact that somebody "desires to be great" and sets out to achieve that goal by following a path of service does not automatically qualify them for the leadership role they seek.

Authority is conferred by God

Again, we learn that it is perfectly acceptable to desire the position of bishop (1 Tim. 3:1), and in the following verse, combined with Titus 1:7, we are given all the necessary characteristics that must appear of the aspiring bishop's CV: "Blameless, the husband of one wife, temperate, sober-minded, of good behaviour, hospitable, able to teach . . . not self-willed, not quick-tempered, not given to wine, not violent, not greedy for money." But as I have said, having "a servant heart" is not of itself a ticket to leadership status, any more than being particularly gifted is a qualification, or even ticking every character box in the job application for Bishop. We learn from Ephesians 4 that the leadership ministries – apostle, prophet, evangelist, pastor, and teacher – are gifts given to the Church by Jesus. Whether or not we seek authority in the church, it can only be conferred by God. Jesus Himself, our ultimate leadership role model, announced Himself by saying, "The Spirit of the Lord is upon Me . . ." (Luke 4:18).

So how do we know if a man or woman is a leader chosen by the Lord? Gifting of itself is not a sign, for we know from

1 Corinthians 14 that the Holy Spirit gives gifts as he chooses. We know that having a servant heart, and even fulfilling all the human qualifications for eldership listed by Paul in the letters to Timothy and Titus are not of themselves enough. For the Church seeking to appoint leaders, I suggest that the key is in Judges 6:34: "The Spirit of the LORD came upon Gideon; then he blew the trumpet, and the Abiezrites gathered behind him." Do people gather to this person because they see that the Holy Spirit is on him? If they do, he can be expected to lead them into victory over the Midianites that they face, because "Father is (his) help". If they don't – look for someone else.

Bible references

Judges 6:34
1 Samuel 16
1 Samuel 24:6
2 Samuel 5:1-3
Mark 10:42-44
1 Timothy 3:2
Titus 1:7
Ephesians 4:11
Luke 4:18
Judges 6:34

Chapter Six
Know Your God: the Fleece

Gideon had met with God, but at this point did not know Him. It is those who know their God who do exploits. The fleece does not show us what to do, but who we are in Christ: filled with the Spirit, and set apart.

The enemy has gathered; they have set up camp in the Valley. Gideon has raised his army: Manasseh, Naphtali, Asher and Zebulun are all behind him. The signal to go into battle – the trumpet – has sounded. Gideon felt the Spirit of the Lord come upon him before he blew the horn, so why wait any longer? The enemy could start their advance any minute. Thirty-two thousand men are clamouring to go into battle before they do.

"Hang on, chaps," says Gideon. "I just need to check that this is right!"

It's easy to imagine the murmuring – "We're here; the enemy is there; the Lord is obviously with us, what's to check?" – but as we know from the verses that follow, the Lord had other plans.

This section of the story is probably the one that is most frequently referred to in the Church, when people are seeking God's will over difficult decisions. Rather like casting lots, we "lay out a fleece" to see if God's will can be discerned through the outcome of events: "I'll do x-y-z, Lord; and if a-b-c happens I'll take that to be a sign from You to go ahead with this plan I'm considering".

In our times it tends to be something of a last resort: if we're not sure that we've heard from God, we "lay out a fleece". It can almost be as if we're twisting the Lord's arm – "God, you've got to answer me now! I've laid out this fleece, and whichever way things turn out I'm going to read Your will into it!" At this point, we have forgotten Isaiah 59:1 – "Surely the arm of the LORD is not too short to save, nor his ear too dull to hear." The arm of the Lord is not too short, nor His ear too dull. If any ears are dull, it will be ours.

The first point about the fleece is that Gideon most definitely has heard from God. Not only has he heard, but he has seen Him face to face and been told that he would not die. He has seen fire from heaven consume his sacrifice. He has felt the anointing of the Holy Spirit come upon him when he blew the trumpet. He has seen the very men who were going to kill him for breaking down the altar to Baal gather behind him, ready to follow him into battle. Gideon cannot be desperate for a sign.

> "So Gideon said to God, 'If You will save Israel by my hand as You have said – look, I shall put a fleece of wool on the threshing floor; if there is dew on the fleece only, and *it is* dry on all the ground, then I shall know that You will save Israel by my hand, as You have said.'"

(Judg. 6:36-37)

Why then, after the power encounter that Gideon had experienced, was Gideon still so uncertain? The answer can be found a few chapters back in the book of Judges, following the death of Joshua.

> "When all that generation had been gathered to their fathers, another generation arose after them who did not know the Lord nor the work which He had done for Israel."

(Judg. 2:10)

Gideon had met the Lord, but he did not know Him. He was one of a succession of judges that the Lord raised up to deliver His people each time they did evil in His sight and turned to the gods of the Canaanite people. Generation after generation, the pattern was repeated: Israel provoked God to anger by turning away from Him and worshipping the Baals; He allowed them to fall into the hands of raiding tribes; they called out to Him in desperation; He took pity on them and raised up a judge for their deliverance. So by the time of Gideon they had already been rescued by Othniel, Ehud and Deborah, but they had learnt nothing, and fallen back into the ways of the people of the land.

Even today, with the empowering help of the indwelling Holy Spirit, how difficult it can be to make a stand for Jesus, and to separate ourselves from the ways of the world around us – even though James tells us clearly that friendship with the world is enmity for those who belong to God.

So Gideon had grown up among a people immersed in godless ways, who knew that Israel had a God who had delivered them in the past and who probably believed that if they cried long and loud enough He would probably deliver them again; but until then they were probably prepared to put up with the hardships they were enduring because the availability of easy pleasure with the people of the land was simply more tempting than seeking the ways of the God of their fathers. When Gideon met with God, he quickly discovered His requirements, but he knew nothing of His character. Asked the question today, "Will God do as He has said?", any Christian will quote verses of scripture to show that if there is one thing we can be certain of about our God, it is that He is faithful, and that He will perform His word. For Gideon, this attribute was hidden. We cannot look at Old Testament encounters with New Testament eyes.

Looking forward prophetically to the days we live in now, Daniel said, "People who know their God shall . . . carry out great exploits" (Dan. 11:32). Gideon was being called to do exploits without the security of that knowledge of Him. At the same time, everything in Scripture is there for our instruction, so we can look at the episode of the fleece and learn from it. Clearly Gideon learnt enough to carry out one of the most famous "exploits" in Old Testament history. I believe that the two occasions of laying out the fleece can help equip us for the exploits that God has planned for us today. The fleeces do not show us what to do: they show us who we are.

Wet fleece, dry ground

"Look, I shall put a fleece of wool on the threshing floor; if there is dew on the fleece only, and *it is* dry on all the ground, then I shall know that You will save Israel by my hand, as You have said."

(Judg. 6:37)

When Gideon rose early the next morning, he found that the fleece was wet and the ground was dry. He wrung a bowlful of water out of it. I have just seen a video of someone being baptised in the sea.

KNOW YOUR GOD: THE FLEECE

He walked out of the waves, and stood on the dry sand, dripping with the waters of his baptism into Christ. Baptism symbolises the death of the old self and the birth of the new creation, immersed in Christ and set apart from the world. In the picture of the wet fleece laid out on the dry threshing floor we have an Old Testament type of baptism, and its significance for the new birth: set apart, filled with the Spirit, and ready to bring living water into the dry places of the world. As well as knowing that He will do as He has said, knowing our God is also knowing what He has already done: that He has not only "raised [Christ] from the dead and seated Him at His right hand in heavenly places" (Eph. 1:20), but that He has also raised us up together with Him (Eph. 2:6), and that in Christ we are seated together with Him in heavenly places as well. We are not only set apart from the world in order to remain uncontaminated by it; we are set apart from the world because, in Christ, we have been seated in Heaven.

In today's world this distinction between the Church and the world is not always apparent. Although, as Jesus said, we are not "of the world", we can sometimes be so immersed in it that it is hard to tell one from the other. Although in some parts the Church is being restored to New Testament values, in others it is not so different from the Israelites of Gideon's day, who knew of the God of their fathers but were married to the world around them – and under assault from it.

Peter writes that we are "a chosen generation, a royal priesthood, a holy nation, His own special people, that you may proclaim the praises of Him who called you out of darkness into His marvellous light" (1 Pet. 2:9). If we are uncertain of the wisdom of a particular choice, and are seeking God's will for the way forward, we need to think about the wet fleece and ask ourselves the question: will those in the dry places of the world see that we are God's special people, or are we just as dry as they are?

The wilderness of Edom

It is easy enough to find ourselves in a place that is as dry as the desert sand. Our first encounter with the prophet Elisha, after he has taken on Elijah's mantle, is when the kings of Judah, Israel and Edom went together to do battle with Moab (the story is in 2 Kings 3). They decided to march by way of a roundabout route, through the wilderness of Edom. We read there was no water, either for the army or their animals. What their reasoning was for taking this route we will not know until that day when we know all things; but we do know that after seven days they realise that they have made a big mistake. How often, when things are going wrong, do we stop in our tracks and realise that we have gone ahead on something without prayer? Jehoshaphat did:

> "But Jehoshaphat said, 'Is there no prophet of the LORD here, that we may inquire of the LORD by him?' So one of the servants of the king of Israel answered and said, 'Elisha the son of Shaphat is here, who poured water on the hands of Elijah.'"
>
> (2 Kgs 3:11)

As with all the events surrounding the life and ministry of Elisha, there are many aspects and layers to this story and much to learn from it; but in the context of Gideon's victory and the picture of the wet fleece, the important element here is that God not only brought water into the dry place, but also used that water to bring about the defeat of the Moabites. If we know our God, we know that He promises to "pour water on him who is thirsty, and floods on the dry ground" (Isa. 44:3). If our streams have dried up, we always know where to turn for living water. Our Elisha, the Lord Jesus, is always with us to bring deliverance.

Paul told the Thessalonians (1 Thess. 5:17) to "pray without ceasing", and he told the Ephesians (Eph. 6:18) to be "praying always with all prayer and supplication in the Spirit". More than most, Paul knew the necessity of a prayerful life, which is why he exhorts us to keep our fleeces wet – to "be (being) filled with the Spirit". This is an imperative that we must not ignore. But that with which we are filled is there to be squeezed out into whatever "bowls" the Lord set before us; not to leech into the dry ground or evaporate in the heat. Jehoshaphat was a godly king, but he was in the company of lesser men, the idolatrous kings of Samaria and Edom; and it was in the wilderness of Edom that he finally came to his senses and turned to the Lord. He had become as dry as the people around him: he had lost his distinctiveness. So as Christians, and particularly those of us whose work means that we spend a lot of time among the lost, let us not come to a halt in the wilderness of Edom, even though grace is there for us when we do: effective spirit-filled ministry requires not only that we lead a prayerful life, but that we maintain a spirit-filled lifestyle, and in doing so retain the conspicuous identity of who we are in Christ.

Wet ground, dry fleece

An old friend from Gloucestershire, whom I see occasionally at prophetic gatherings, had a vision recently. In the vision she heard the sound of an old-fashioned typewriter, very loud, filling the room with the clack-clack-clack sound of the keys on the paper. Then she saw the typewriter, an old black upright machine. According to the way she told the story, there was no hand actually on the typewriter, but words were being formed. Instead of coming out of the top, the paper was coming out of the side, so the message was creating a banner. It said – this was in normal sized type –

"Some of my people are living dangerously"

Then in very large letters, the single word: **MIXTURE**

Some of us are mixing the flesh and the spirit; the Kingdom of God and the kingdoms of the world. Perhaps a public ministry – and a little bit of private sin. Declaring God's faithfulness – and being faithless in marriage. God in our Sunday conversations and in our quiet times – and a critical spirit and judgemental tongue for those close to us at other times. There are many ways of living this mixture, but there is only one truth: "the flesh lusts against the Spirit, and the Spirit against the flesh; and these are contrary to one another" (Gal. 5:17).

Isaiah exhorts God's people (Isa. 48:20) to "Go forth from Babylon", and many scholars read this as being an exhortation to be separate from the world's systems. Looking to the book of Revelation, when the cry goes out from the third angel that "Babylon has fallen", we read that anyone who receives the mark of the beast "shall also drink of the wine of the wrath of God" (Rev. 14:10). There is no certain interpretation of these scriptures, but one thing is clear: as God's chosen people we have been called out of the world, its systems and its ways; out of darkness and into the "marvellous light" of the Lord Jesus. Anything that is not separation is mixture, and God tells us that mixture is dangerous. And so, from the other side, we come back to the fleece, which on the second night was not touched by the water all around it.

If we are searching the Scriptures for promises of divine protection, the first stop for many of us is likely to be Psalm 91, which begins with the wonderful words: "He who dwells in the secret place of the Most High shall abide under the shadow of the Almighty." In Psalm 91 we find promises of protection from many forms of untimely death, we find angels keeping us from harm, we find deliverance, salvation and long life in our God. When He is our refuge, nothing "out there" can touch our fleece. But we do have to read all these promises of refuge in the context of the first line. God's love is unconditional. God's grace is unconditional. Salvation is by grace and not by works, "lest anyone should boast" (Eph. 2:9). The cross is unconditional. Yet many of God's promises still require our response if we are to find their ultimate fulfilment: to receive all the protection that the secret place of the Most High affords, we do need to dwell there; and we cannot bring the ways of the world and the lusts of the flesh into the refuge with us.

If we look at the conquest of Jericho again we can see that this principle also is illustrated in that famous victory: when Joshua led the Israelites across the Jordan he knew that the Jericho lay before them – he would not have been unaware of it on his spying trip forty years previously. But the preparation that God had in mind for the battle ahead was not fitness training or weapons drill: it was circumcision. We read in Joshua 5 how he took flint knives and circumcised the army, who stayed in the camp until they were healed. Any enemy falling upon this vulnerable group of men would have probably annihilated them, but this was a consecrated army in obedience to God: they were truly dwelling "in the secret place of the Most High", and thus they were invincible. And when they moved out into battle, their obedience alone was enough to cause the walls to fall.

So in the two episodes of the fleece we see a man called to do exploits, but who did not know his God; and we see ourselves, the sheep of His pasture, who do know our God, but on the whole do not do many exploits. And we see our God, revealing Himself to Gideon and to the Church. He says: "Do you want My power? Soak yourselves in my Spirit. Do you want My protection? Consecrate yourselves."

So next time we consider "laying out a fleece", we need to remember that the fleece doesn't show us what to do; it shows us who we are in Christ. Gideon moved on from here. Let us walk with him to the River.

Bible references

Isaiah 59:1

Judges 6:36-37

Judges 2:10

Daniel 11:32

Ephesians 1:20

Ephesians 2:6

1 Peter 2:9

2 Kings 3:11

Isaiah 44:3

1 Thessalonians 5:17

Ephesians 6:18

Galatians 5:17

Isaiah 48:20

Revelation 14:10

Psalm 91:1

Ephesians 2:9

Chapter Seven
By Faith (Not by Might, Nor by Power)

Gideon had to go into battle in his weakness, establishing once and for all the principles that we can achieve nothing in our own strength, and that to seek any glory on Earth is to deny God what is His alone. The mature, victorious Christian life involves recognising this truth and staying close to the river of God, drinking from it constantly.

"**A**nd the LORD said to Gideon, 'The people who are with you are too many for Me to give the Midianites into their hands, lest Israel claim glory for itself against Me, saying, "My own hand has saved me."'" (Judg. 7:2)

Gideon had 32,000 men at his command. Whether that army was large enough to defeat the amassed Midianites we will never know, because God had other ideas. We have noted in an earlier chapter that His agenda is not the same as Gideon's. The Israelites wanted deliverance from the invading army; the Lord, then as now, wanted His land cleansed of idolatry. It is easy to pass over the word "against" in verse 2, quoted above: if Israel defeated the Midianites by their own hand, God is saying that they would simply be substituting one form of idolatry with another.

If we pride ourselves in our achievements, we are not just ignoring God, or "leaving Him out of the equation"; we are actively setting ourselves up against him. The Earth is the Lord's, and all that is in it. Everything we have and do, everything in creation, comes from Him and is for Him – but the temptation to think otherwise is recorded as early as the eleventh chapter of Genesis, in the story of Babel. The purpose of building the tower was to erect "a monument to our greatness" that would "bring us together and keep us from scattering all over the world" (Gen. 11:4 NLT). The builders of that first tower, along with so many other monuments to human achievement that have been set up since then, were competing with God for glory. God intervened at Babel; and we can see other times through history where other monuments to our greatness – the "unsinkable" *Titanic*, for example – appear to have been brought low.

So before Gideon goes into battle, God establishes a principle that holds true for every battle we face: "It is My hand that will save you; not your own." We ignore this at our peril. Whether we are engaged in great projects that push forward the boundaries of science and engineering; or whether we are simply working at our everyday tasks, be it in church or the workplace, we are in a battle twenty-four hours a day, seven days a week. Our own strength, however great it is, will ultimately fail us. As the psalmist says, if the Lord does not build the house, the labourers labour in vain.

Is everything we do covered in prayer? Do we think, like Gideon with his 32,000 men, that we have all the resources that we need at our disposal? If we do, not only are we fooling ourselves and are making ourselves vulnerable to attack, but, more seriously, we are setting ourselves up "against" God. He is the one who wants the glory for our achievements. We may ask ourselves at times: "Why is this? Why should God want all the glory for Himself? Why will He not share it?" One reason is that to do so would be untruthful, and since God is Truth He cannot allow it. All things are from Him and for Him, so everything bears His signature. He really cannot give His glory to another. As the apostle Paul exhorts us: "Whether you eat or drink *or whatever you do*, do it all for the glory of God" (1 Cor. 10:31).

You can go home

Gideon's first instruction seems to be a very "unspiritual" one — "Send everyone home who is timid or afraid". In His grace God meets us where we are. He consistently tells us to "Fear not", yet He doesn't stand over us with a stick and say "You should have more faith!" Faith is a gift from God, and it is His faith that He gives us, not our faith that we drum up. It can be easy to fall into the trap of being over-zealous when we think we are being spiritual, and operating "in faith" in our own strength when the Holy Spirit hasn't actually told us that it is time to throw away the crutches, or stop taking the medication and believe for divine healing. The result can be very damaging. When we were still young Christians Anne had digestive problems which had been with her for years. I consistently told her that she should "have more faith", when actually I hadn't heard that specifically from the Lord and I should have encouraged her to go to the doctor – "You can go home; you don't have to fight this battle." When she was much later diagnosed with a hiatus hernia, the negative impact of my zealous intolerance had probably scarred our relationship as much as it had scarred her oesophagus, and now, even though she has had surgery, Anne is still on medication.

God may provide all we need for life and godliness (2 Pet. 1:3), and by His stripes we were most certainly healed; but He only asks that we live out our Christian lives according to "the measure of faith" that He has "dealt us" (Rom. 12:3). In the matter of giving, Paul says to the Corinthians: "If there is first a willing mind, it is accepted according to what one has, and not according to what he doesn't have" (2 Cor. 8:12), and I think the testimony of Scripture is that this principle is true in all areas of faith. God wants us to grow in every area; He wants us to stand, to be strong, and to press on towards the goal of the upward call of God in Christ Jesus. But He also says to us that if we are too weak or fearful for the battle today, it's OK – we can go home. We are not condemned, and we are not deserters.

Twenty-two thousand men gratefully left Mount Gilead; 10,000 remained. As the battle lines thinned out, what was Gideon thinking? It was probably something like: "Thank you Lord! That lot wouldn't have been much use to me. Now I know I have warriors I can rely on . . ." He probably imagined his valiant company wading into the enemy, terrorising them with their fearlessness, slaying them in their droves and putting the rest to flight. Whatever he did think as two-thirds of his army headed back down the hill, we can probably be sure that he was not expecting the next selection process. As we know, God's thoughts are not our thoughts, and His ways are not our ways.

Go to the River

One of the songs that came out the 1994 "Toronto Blessing" time of refreshing was "The River is Here". The River, of course, is the River of God, the River of the Holy Spirit. "All who linger on this river's shore, will end up thirsting for more of the Lord" runs the song. We know that nothing ventured without God is bound to fail, and that, since our battle is not "*against flesh and blood*, but *against principalities*, *against* powers, *against* the rulers of the darkness of this age" (Eph. 6:12), we can only expect victory through prayer and the power of the Spirit. Whether or not we embrace charismatic theology in our understanding of the operation of the presence, gifts and power of the Holy Spirit in the Church today, it makes sense symbolically that God should instruct Gideon to go down to the river before engaging battle with the enemy.

We see the fullest depiction of God's river in Ezekiel 47:1,12:

> "Then he brought me back to the door of the temple; and there was water, flowing from under the threshold of the temple toward the east, for the front of the temple faced east; the water was flowing from under the right side of the temple, south of the altar . . . Along the bank of the river, on this side and that, will grow all *kinds of* trees used for food; their leaves will not wither, and their fruit will not fail. They will bear fruit every month, because their water flows from the sanctuary. Their fruit will be for food, and their leaves for medicine."

Most of us will have read this passage, probably several times, and received teaching from it. Some of us will testify to having spent time in its refreshing waters. Knowingly or unknowingly, all of us thirst for them. The river flows from the place of the throne of God, bringing healing and life out into the world. Ezekiel was instructed to go ever deeper until the water was too deep for him to cross, and we find here a picture of the Church being called to move deeper into God, from the place of paddling to the place where we are "out of our depth" and reliant totally on Him.

I think a salient point in this passage is that the river gets deeper as it flows away from the Temple. We have a tendency in the Church to think in terms of going "deeper into God" in our worship meetings and prayer times: we seek to immerse ourselves in Him as we approach the throne in worship – then as soon as we turn our backs on the altar, and, in the terms of Ezekiel 47, "face East" in the direction of the River's flow, we promptly step out onto dry ground. The biblical picture is actually the opposite: the further away we go from the Temple, the more deeply we should be immersed.

Hand to mouth

So it is here, at the river, that God finally reduced the remaining 10,000 men to the 300 who would deliver Israel under Gideon and give glory to the Lord.

> "So he brought the people down to the water. And the LORD said to Gideon, 'Everyone who laps from the water with his tongue, as a dog laps, you shall set apart by himself; likewise everyone who gets down on his knees to drink.'"

(Judg. 7:5)

I remember my early – and not so early – years as a Christian, lurching from one crisis to another, practically counting off the days till the next church meeting because I couldn't wait to get down to the River. Dry as dust, I would sing "As the deer pants for the water, so my soul longs after You . . .", then I'd get down onto my knees and plunge my face into the waters and drink of the refreshing stream. I'd go to a Bible convention, lap up the teaching, go forward for ministry, feel the presence of God and be touched by the Holy Spirit – then a week later nothing would have changed. For years the power of God washed over me, again and again; but there was no power in my life. I was not one of the 300.

Since Gideon's time, very little has changed among the people of God: thousands come to the River, but only a few can truly be said to be putting the enemy to flight. All too often, being at the River is the end of the journey: we go to the River – the one flowing East, away from the temple, that Ezekiel saw – put our mouths in the water to drink, and walk away until we're thirsty again. This is not maturity; this is ministry addiction. Maturity is putting our cupped hands into the River, drawing from the unlimited supply of the Spirit, and making that portion of it our own. It is Christ in us, not Christ in Heaven, that is the hope of Glory. Of course we can't walk far with water in our cupped hands; we leak, we spill, and we keep having to go back – which is why the verb in Ephesians 5:18 – "be filled with the Spirit" – is in the present continuous: "Be being filled". We have to keep going back. But the difference between the mature 300 and the rest is that while they are by the river (and we should always be close to the River) they are drawing on the "supply of the Spirit of Jesus Christ" (Phil. 1:19) that is their own, not receiving it from someone else's ministry.

When teaching his disciples faith, Jesus said; "Therefore I tell you, whatever you ask for in prayer, *believe* that you have *received* it, and it will be yours" (Mark 11:24 NIV). Jesus asks us not just to go to the River to pray, but to cup our hands, receive the answer that is there in the Spirit, flowing down from the throne of God, and take it away for ourselves. The Holy Spirit is given to us a "deposit guaranteeing our inheritance until the redemption of those who are God's possession – to the praise of his glory" (Eph. 1:14). God wants us to take hold of our portion.

So how do we keep our hands to our mouths?

Consider the picture now: the mature Christian, walking close to the River (fellowshipping with the Holy Spirit), repeatedly stooping down to refill his cupped hands (being filled with the Holy Spirit) and take a drink (in faith receiving the answers to his or her prayers). Smith Wigglesworth was "The Apostle of Faith". He saw multitudes of souls saved; many great healings; the dead raised. He would certainly be counted among the 300. One day, his friend's car ran out of petrol. Wigglesworth instructed him to pour water into the petrol tank. He did so; the car coughed a few times then started, and when, later, it was inspected by a mechanic, nothing but pure petrol was found in the engine.

Smith Wigglesworth's ministry was based on four principles:

1. Read the word of God.
2. Consume the word until it consumes you.
3. Believe the word.
4. Act on it.

To what extent do we live by these four principles?

Many of us are like the car that Wigglesworth was travelling in. We roll along with our tank nearly empty, then wonder why we come to a bumping halt and need a miracle to start again. We "do our daily reading", maybe – but what does that consist of? All too often it's 15 minutes spent on a few verses and somebody else's notes. It's a bit of petrol sloshing in the bottom of our tank: it might keep us going for a few miles, and for whatever our journey is in the routine of our day – but it isn't going to take us into battle. We might say, "Yes, but not many people are called to that level of ministry – I have a job – I have a family – I have children – We have to hold all these in balance," etc. These are all realities, and God knows all of our lives and how much room there is in our tanks. But the fact is that when we face the battle it is not usually because we have gone out looking for it; it is because the Midianites have arrived unannounced, threatening our jobs, our families, our children; threatening the very areas of our lives that we say are keeping us from being consumed with the word. The question we have to answer is this: when we read the word, does it stay with us through the day? Do we draw on it like a car draws on the petrol in its tank? Is it what drives, shapes and motivates us? Or does it drift to the back of our minds, buried under our responsibilities and preoccupations?

Throughout Scripture, the Holy Spirit consistently reminds us that God is unsearchable. Whether admonishing Job, the wisest man of his generation, for "[darkening] counsel by words without knowledge" (Job 3:2), or crying out through Paul that the Church would grasp "the exceeding greatness of His power toward us who believe" (Eph. 1:19), the message is repeated again and again that we cannot limit God with our thinking. Probably the best-known of these passages is Isaiah 55:8-9:

> "For My thoughts are not your thoughts, nor are your ways My ways . . . as the heavens are higher than the earth, so are My ways higher than your ways and My thoughts than your thoughts."

We cannot "work it out" – but we can reach to Him for revelation, and His word, the *rhema* word breathed to us now by His Spirit, will carry His weight in our situations. So He says in Jeremiah 23:29, "Is not My word like a fire . . . and like a hammer that breaks a rock in pieces?", and finishes the message to Isaiah by affirming that, even though we cannot reach His thinking, His word can, and will, reach us:

> "As the rain and the snow come down from heaven, and do not return to it without watering the earth and making it bud and flourish, so that it yields seed for the sower and bread for the eater, so is my word that goes out from my mouth: it will not return to me empty, but will accomplish what I desire and achieve the purpose for which I sent it."

(Isaiah 55:10-11 NIV)

Jesus teaches that the Kingdom of God is like a grain of mustard seed, which grows to be the biggest plant in the garden until it's a tree that the birds come and roost in (Matt. 13:31-32), or like yeast which transforms 60 lbs of dough into loaves of bread. The difference between His thoughts and ours, His ways and ours is as great as the distance between Heaven and Earth (Isaiah 55:9). Even when we see the Word that goes out of His mouth, our human perception can only see the mustard seed. Yet within the life in that seed is a tree that houses the birds of the air. Within the yeast is the life that makes the bread. We need eyes of faith to see the tree within the seed if we want the Kingdom of God to break out in our midst, and the lifeless dough of our experience transformed into loaves of heavenly bread. The purpose for which God sends His word is always far higher than our minds can grasp.

Most of us will have heard or read teaching from Ephesians 6 on the armour of God; we know that the sword of the Spirit is the word of God, and we have probably heard that it is the only offensive weapon in Paul's list. But when the Midianites are upon us and we need a weapon, where do our instincts take us? Do we reach for our sword, the Word of God – or do we reach for words of anger, do we hide in fear, do we flounder in desperation? This is the litmus test of how we are reading the Word. Are we reading it because we recognise that there is nothing more important that we are going to do in the day (other than praying, which is at the same level of importance), or are we reading it because "it's what we do"? We can read three chapters of the Bible and forget about them five minutes later (empty tank), or we can read three verses and keep them in mind all day (full tank). We need to treat our Bible reading the same way as we treat "that thing I have to do this afternoon": we use a strategy of our choice to keep it uppermost in our minds. What strategy do we use to keep today's scripture uppermost in our minds?

The word of God is living and active. It is God's word that penetrates our circumstances and injects them with His limitless creative power. If we are active with it, we will know its activity in our lives. By continually giving it pre-eminence we will be consumed by it. And when we are sufficiently consumed by the Word, we will start to really believe that its truth is more dependable than the appearance of nature and circumstance. Our perception of the laws of science becomes subjugated to faith, which understands "that the universe was formed at God's command, so that what is seen was not made out of what was visible" (Hebrews 11:3 NIV). That the tree is in the seed. Petrol, like wine, can be created from water. We are no longer dependent on circumstances, because circumstances are dependent on a God who is "alert and active, watching over My word to perform it" (Jer. 1:12 AMP).

God is intent on performing His living, active word; actively seeking to break into human life with His creative power. Consistently, Jesus taught that the Kingdom of God is at hand. He didn't look at the seed; He saw the tree. Do we have our portion? Are we focused and intent, with our hands cupped and our hearts and minds full? Are we among the 300?

Bible references

Judges 7:2

Genesis 11:4

1 Corinthians 10:31

2 Peter 1:3

Romans 12:3

2 Corinthians 8:12

Ephesians 6:12

Ezekiel 47:1,12

Judges 7:5

Ephesians 5:18

Philippians 1:19

Mark 11:24

Ephesians 1:14

Job 28:2-7

Ephesians 1:19

Isaiah 55:8-9

Jeremiah 23:29

Isaiah 55:10-11

Matthew 13:31-32

Isaiah 55:9

Hebrews 11:3

Jeremiah 1:12

Chapter Eight
Lessons of the Tongue (1)

The biblical foundation and the value of praying in tongues — dipping our tongues into the water, like the 300. As the systems and resources of the world fall increasingly under the corrupting and destroying power of the enemy, we will need increasingly to rely on the supernatural gifting of the Holy Spirit for our needs to be met.

Smith Wigglesworth, the "Apostle of Faith", is rightly counted among "God's generals". He was a man who kept his cupped hands to his mouth. He died in 1947, when evangelist P.S. Rambabu had not yet been born. In *Dare to Win*, Rambabu writes:

"In another city in England, Bradford, I stood near the grave of Smith Wigglesworth, a man of God who had lived there and been used by God in a powerful way. I was very much inspired by his life and his faith in my early Christian life. The grave bore the epitaph: 'Here lies the man of God Smith Wigglesworth'. But I said to my wife: 'Smith Wigglesworth is dead. It is now, I will arise.' Smith Wigglesworth, John Wesley, Kathryn Kuhlman, and countless other people mightily used by God in their time, are now history, and God is telling us it is our time to do something for Him."

Rambabu has seen many healings, signs and wonders and souls saved through his ministry, and he attributes this fruitfulness in part to the time he spends before the Lord in preparation, praying in tongues. This chapter looks at the place of praying in tongues in the equipping of the warrior. I am of course fully aware that there are many in the body of Christ who are firmly convinced that it has no place at all; and that there are many churches that hold to a cessationist doctrine. Yet others may be seeking the gift of tongues and are at a loss to understand why it has not been granted them, while there are others, committed, worshipping, praying Christians full of the love of God, with no particular doctrinal bias, but for whom the entire charismatic experience is still an unopened book. From the perspective that is formed from my own experience, the testimony of others and my understanding of Scripture, praying in tongues is a gift of the Holy Spirit that God has made available to equip and build up the Church, and from this point on I will treat it as one of the "essentials" in the armoury of the warrior.

In 1 Corinthians 14:4 Paul declares that we "edify ourselves" when we speak in an unknown tongue. The word he uses means, literally, to build upwards, as a building is built up from the foundations. The same root can be found in Jude 1:20, where we are exhorted to build ourselves up in our faith by praying in the Spirit. I don't believe that "praying in the Holy Spirit" always means praying in tongues, but I do believe that sometimes it does. Paul and Jude, therefore, both consider that praying in tongues is one means that is given to us for "building ourselves up". When Jesus says that He will build His Church (Matt. 16:18) it is the same word that is used again. In Ephesians 4, Paul writes of how the five-fold ministries are given to the Church for equipping and "edifying" – building up – the body of Christ until we all reach the stature of the fullness of Christ. The finished building, the Church, will be the perfected, unified, spirit-filled body of Christ on Earth; the Temple where the presence of God will dwell. Whoever we are building up, whether ourselves or others, it is for the purpose of becoming more like Christ: not just to be more like Him in character, but also to be more like Him in our actions, as we do those "greater things" that He promises in John 14:12. Jesus gave the gift of tongues to the Church so that we could participate more fully in His building programme.

Martin's heel

I have been a Christian now since 1983. A prominent name associated with the healing ministry then, as now, was Ian Andrews. At one "Bible week" seminar I attended not many years after I was saved I remember him talking about the value of praying in tongues, and I left the meeting resolved to spend more time doing just that. One thing he had mentioned was that God could bring a word of knowledge as an interpretation of a tongue, and that the interpretation might not follow immediately after the tongue, but possibly after an interval of several hours. I was a schoolteacher at the time, and it took me about 40 minutes to drive to school in the mornings. I decided I would spend that time praying in tongues, and that I would try and be open to any interpretation the Holy Spirit might bring in the course of the day. I was as keen to witness as I was immature, and I am sure I left a number of students very perplexed at some of the "words of knowledge" that my imagination cooked up during those heady times. But there were also a few occasions when it did seem that I had heard from the Lord. One in particular was when I was covering for a games lesson. It was my least favourite subject, and I was glad to be given the task of looking after the students who had some sort of minor injury which meant that they were unable to participate in the lesson. I recognised one of them: he was actually a Christian himself. In a lesson where I had taught him earlier that term, I had told the class about my faith (it was much easier in those days!), and he had approached me at the end and given me a slip of paper with the Bible verse John 14:2 written on it. I was really blessed: it was the first time I had been "given a word" by anyone, and it came from a 13-year-old boy. We'll call him Martin.

The games teacher asked for the children to bring him their notes. As Martin handed his over, the Holy Spirit spoke to me. He said, "It's his foot." When he came back to his place, I spoke to him. The conversation went a bit like this:

"It's your foot, isn't it?"

"Yes, it is. How do you know?"

"God just told me, when you handed in your note. I believe He's going to heal you. What's the problem, anyway?"

"It's this. I can't run. Look."

I had been expecting a sprained ankle or similar. He told me he had a raw place on the back of his heel where a nasty blister had burst, just where the edge of his trainers would rub. By now we were outside, and the rest of the class, except for one other classmate who was also with us and looking on with interest, were gathered at the far end of the playing fields. I placed my hand on the back of his foot and just said, "Be healed, in Jesus' name," and told him to run to a certain spot about 20 yards away, which he did. The pain had gone. When he rolled down his sock to have a look, so had the blister. His friend said: "That's cool!' (or whatever they said at that time). 'Can you pray for me as well? I've got asthma." I prayed for him, and commanded the asthma to go. We went back inside after the lesson, and that was the end of it. I left the school soon after that, and didn't see much of either of them again until four or five years later, when I bumped into Martin at a Christian concert in the town. He asked me if I remembered praying for his friend, which of course I did. Apparently he never suffered from asthma again after that day.

I am not someone with a "healing ministry", but I have at times seen healings when I have prayed. (I have also seen no healing on numerous occasions!) But I will always remember that grey morning and Martin's heel. Yes, it was only a blister. But one minute it was there, and then it wasn't. It hurt, and then it didn't. I saw God create the visible (healed skin) from the invisible: whether it is a blister, or cancer, the miracle is essentially no different in nature (although obviously very different in outcome for the sufferer). Jesus tells us that the sick "will be healed" if we lay hands on them. Ever since that experience, I have always been prepared to pray for healing; and as I have said, there have been occasions where I have seen that healing manifest, and Jesus has been glorified as a result. I am convinced that there is a connection between the timing of that word of knowledge and the time I had spent praying in tongues on the way into school. It most definitely built me up in my faith.

The cash buyer and praying in tongues

Another occasion that stands out as an example of the power of sustained praying in tongues is more recent, and in an entirely different context. Anne and I had bought a "buy to let" property just before a period when house prices rose sharply. The house we bought was priced lower than market value because there was a sitting tenant. Because we needed tenants, this was not a problem for us; just the opposite in fact, as it meant that we were receiving some income from the outset. However, it was less than a couple of years before we decided that we weren't cut out for the property business, so we decided to put the house on the market again. The value had risen steeply, so we were set for a tidy financial blessing. But there was a problem: we still had the same sitting tenant. Coupled with the fact that prices had now peaked, this meant that nobody was interested in buying our house.

It was during this time that we watched a Rambabu video, in which he taught on praying in tongues; in particular the power of praying in tongues persistently. One morning Anne felt a strong desire to start praying, and she spent about an hour praying in tongues, lifting up the house situation to the Lord. At around midday there was a phone call: it was the estate agents. "Can you come into the office now, please? We have a cash buyer interested in your property, and he would like to have a look around."

Not only did he buy, but he paid our asking price.

There seems to be a resurgence of cessationist doctrine in the Church today, which denies the operation of charismatic gifts in the Church. The position of one well-respected "moderate cessationist", when writing about guidance, is that God won't supernaturally whisper in our ear "which stocks to pick", but that our guidance will come as the image of Jesus becomes clearer and brighter through the work of the Holy Spirit in our lives and in our study of the Scriptures (see *Every Good Endeavour* by Timothy Keller). Paul writes to the Romans: "Likewise the Spirit also helps in our weaknesses. For we do not know what we should pray for as we ought, but the Spirit Himself makes intercession for us with groanings which cannot be uttered" (Rom. 8:26). I would say that Anne did not know how to pray for our house sale, but the Holy Spirit did. Was some angelic intervention necessary in heavenly places? How was our buyer led to the advert for our house? We will never know, but we do know that Anne prayed in tongues and he turned up at the estate agent's. The Holy Spirit didn't exactly whisper which stocks to pick, but as Anne spent that time in close fellowship with Him He clearly had a direct influence on our finances.

I am of course totally sold-out on the image of Jesus becoming ever clearer and brighter in my life, but I think the cessationists miss the main blessing of praying in tongues: that as we do so, particularly over a longer period of time rather than a quick utterance a few seconds long, we increase our awareness of the presence and power of the Holy Spirit within us, and as this happens we are able to submit our thoughts and emotions to Him. On many occasions I have found myself yielding my thoughts and my emotions to temptation – for example when I am in the car, on my own on the motorway, and my mind is wandering. I can say hand on heart that every time I have caught myself in that dangerous place and have prayed in tongues, the temptation has left and my thought-life has returned to the light. James exhorts us to submit to God and resist the devil (Jas. 4:7). In my experience, praying in tongues when temptation comes is a good way of doing just that.

God led Gideon and his men to the water to call out a band of warriors. He knew that the power and the victory was His and His alone, so His one and only priority was to "pick a team" who would be completely obedient to His will. It appears as we read today's news that the influence of the enemy and the fulfilment of his all-consuming desire to kill, steal and destroy is increasing daily. As financial bastions crumble, the Church will increasingly need supernatural guidance to be able to find the funding that will finance end-time revival – and that could well include being told supernaturally "which stocks to pick" – after all, they are all His anyway. One day systems will fail and medicines will run out, and when that day comes people will come to Jesus for healing. When darkness increasingly covers the earth, the Church will need to depend more and more on the "pillar of cloud by day and the fire by night" to keep "shining like stars in the midst of a crooked and perverse generation as we hold out the word of life" (see Phil. 2:15-16). We seek not the gift, but the Gift Giver. If we honour and value the presence and person of the Holy

Spirit within us and within each other, if we continually seek to fellowship with Him, we will only have one agenda: the glory and the Kingdom of God. We need to keep on dipping our tongues in the living water of the Holy Spirit, constantly replenishing our supply as we keep ourselves close to the stream.

Bible references

1 Corinthians 14:4
Jude 1:20
Matthew 16:18
John 14:12
Romans 8:26
James 4:7
Philippians 2:15-16

Chapter Nine
Lessons of the Tongue (2)

Just as the supernatural gift of tongues is given to us for our own edification, so our natural use of the tongue should only be used for the edification of others. There is no place in the Kingdom of God for the use of idle, negative words.

There is a corollary to the material dealt with in the preceding chapter. Chapter eight deals with the words in an unknown language that our tongues speak when "given utterance" (Acts 2:4) by the Holy Spirit. Before leaving the River, however, I'd like to reflect briefly on the words that we, as warriors, will choose not to speak; the image of keeping our hands to our mouths as one of controlling what comes out of them as well as cupping what goes in.

David writes: "Let the words of my mouth and the meditation of my heart be acceptable in Your sight, O LORD, my strength and my Redeemer" (Ps. 19:14).

The psalmist knew the importance of the words we speak. God admonished Job for uttering "words without knowledge". Proverbs is studded with wisdom on the importance of holding one's tongue and the folly of babble. Jesus raises the stakes, and tells us (Matt. 12:36-37): "But I say to you that for every idle word men may speak, they will give account of it in the day of judgement. For by your words you will be justified, and by your words you will be condemned."

When is a word "idle"? The Greek word is *argos*. The Strong's definition is "lazy, shunning the labour which one ought to perform", or "free from labour; at leisure". Idle words are those spoken when, to use the vernacular, "you open your mouth without engaging your brain". Proverbs 18:21 tells us that "Death and life are in the power of the tongue". James tells us that we can put a bit in the mouth of a horse, we can steer a ship by its rudder, but that no man can control the tongue, yet in the same letter – almost in the same breath – he makes it clear that it is absolutely necessary to do so.

How do we reconcile these two opposites? We find the solution, to this as to so many other riddles, in Romans 7:24-25, where Paul famously writes:

"O wretched man that I am! Who will deliver me from this body of death? I thank God – through Jesus Christ our Lord! So then, with the mind I myself serve the law of God, but with the flesh the law of sin."

Elsewhere Paul exhorts us to take "every thought into captivity to the obedience of Christ" (2 Cor. 10:5). Idle words – words spoken without putting the brain to work – are words of the flesh that serve "the law of sin". Jesus, however, spoke only words of life: every thought that passed through His mind was taken captive to serve the Law of God. He was the living fulfilment of Proverbs 15:4, which tells us that a "wholesome" (a word with a root meaning of healing, cure, deliverance) tongue is a tree of life. The same verse goes on to tell us that perverseness (meaning subversion, ruin) in it breaks the spirit. We have "the mind of Christ" – with our tongue submitted to His mind we speak from the tree of life. The word 'idle' is in the middle of unbridled: idle and unbridled, the tongue, as James puts it, is set on fire by Hell. Death and life are in the power of the tongue; we are justified or condemned by our words.

Controlling the tongue does not come naturally: it involves work – Strong's word "labour" – to be submitted and avoid idle words. How often do we say something negative or hurtful, and then try and cover up by saying "It was only a joke" or "I didn't mean it"? Do you know anyone who will preface some negative or contradictory statement by saying "I don't want to be negative (or contradictory), BUT . . ." then goes on to say something that he has just told you that he didn't want to say (i.e. a negative comment), and finishes by apologising for what he has said? A lot of words are spoken for effect. Christians are by no means immune to this temptation. Do any of us know a Miss (Mr, or Mrs) Idwtbnb (I Don't Want To Be Negative But . . .)? Miss Idwtbnb is aware of the negativity of her words, but is emotionally dependent on the attention she will get from saying them, or from the satisfaction that an unredeemed, unsubmitted part of her psyche gets from the put-down. So she thinks she can retract the words after she has milked them for their effect. Unfortunately words, as my wife often reminds me, cannot be taken back. Just as the words that go forth from God's mouth will fulfil their purpose, so all the words that we speak will fulfil a purpose – for life, or for death. If there had been cars in the days of the first apostles, I am fairly certain that James would have used a car image in his "horse's bit / ship's rudder" analogy. Just like when driving a car, we need to be in complete control of where our tongue is heading. If we are not, we are going to crash – damaging ourselves and others, fulfilling Proverbs 13:3: "He who guards his mouth preserves his life, but he who opens wide his lips shall have destruction."

It is not just the wisdom literature that conveys this message in the Old Testament: there are two stories in particular that illustrate its importance. The first one I want to look at is the story of Elisha in 2 Kings 2, where he takes up the mantle of Elijah. There is much we can learn from this account, but what is significant in the context of "keeping our hands to our mouths" to control the tongue is the interaction between Elisha and the groups of prophets ("the sons of the prophets") both at Bethel and at Jericho. On each occasion they asked the same question – Did he know that Elijah will be taken from him today? – and both times Elisha said, yes, he did know, and he forbade them to speak.

Elisha knew exactly what was happening – he may not have had a revelation of the Where or the When, but he certainly knew the What. He knew exactly what he wanted from God, and he was going to pursue it single-mindedly. He wanted words of life, or nothing. He knew that the sons of the prophets were not about to give him words of life, so he refused to receive from them at all. Interestingly, they recognised that the anointing was on Elisha when he crossed back over the Jordan (who wouldn't have?), yet they were not prepared to embrace the new move of God's Spirit that came with it: instead they insisted on going up into the mountains to see if they could find Elijah. They wanted to hold onto the past. If we want to move on in our walk with God, defeating our Midianites and advancing the Kingdom, we need to renounce speaking negative words over our circumstances.

The other famous story of zipped mouths is of course the defeat of Jericho, which we find in Joshua 6:1-27. Verse 10 tells us: "Now Joshua had commanded the people, saying, 'You shall not shout or make any noise with your voice, nor shall a word proceed out of your mouth, until the day I say to you, "Shout!" Then you shall shout.'" For six days they marched round the walls with the trumpets sounding and their lips sealed. We know from Ephesians 6 that our battle is not with flesh and blood, but with the spiritual powers of darkness in the heavenly realms. Clearly every battle fought by the Israelites was spiritual in nature, and in a number of instances there are angelic beings working out God's purposes against His enemies. But nowhere else do we see the Lord turning up in person to lead His army, as we do in chapter 5 verse 14. The presence of the Commander of the Lord's army lifts "zipping it" onto a higher level altogether.

Jesus makes it clear (Matt. 11:12) that we do not drift passively into the kingdom of heaven; rather we press into the Kingdom, and seize our prize. Satan stole our inheritance in the Garden of Eden, and there are times when we need to wrestle it away from him. Even Jesus didn't always just snap His fingers, or, as Namaan expected of the prophet he had been sent to, just "wave his hand over the spot" – at different times He groaned in the Spirit and wept (John 11 – the raising of Lazarus), He had to persevere with ministry before the blind man could see more than "trees walking" (Mark 8:24), and He tells us in Matthew 17:21 of the demons that only "come out by prayer and fasting". When we are taking ground *for* the Kingdom of God, we do well to remember that we are also taking it *from* the kingdom of darkness. We are in a battle zone. So as the first battle-ground in the taking of the Promised Land, the fall of Jericho gives us an important picture of how to conduct our warfare: moving under God's direction to the accompaniment of praise, we keep our lips sealed until we give the victory shout.

No corrupt word

Paul gives us some very clear direction in the letter to the Ephesians 4:29: "Let no corrupt word proceed out of your mouth, but what is good for necessary edification, that it may impart grace to the hearers." *No* corrupt word. *Only* what is good. Why? In order to "impart grace". The meaning of the Greek word for corrupt, σαπρός (*sapros*) is rotten, putrefied, unfit for use, worthless. Jesus has one over-arching purpose on this Earth, and we are called to be part of it: it is to build His Church as the vehicle for extending the Kingdom of God. If our words are full of grace, they edify, and His purpose is furthered. Idle words, however, are unchecked and uncontrolled. They do not express the mind of Christ, and will bring rottenness and destruction.

We are a redeemed people, bought at the price of the blood of the Lamb. God delights in using the foolish things of the world to "shame the wise" (1 Cor. 1:27). His strength is made perfect in our weakness (2 Cor. 12:9). Very often this can mean that the very areas in our lives which were most ravaged by sin in our unredeemed self are the areas in which He is most glorified when they are submitted to His purposes. I write these words on controlling the tongue in the knowledge that my uncontrolled tongue has for many years, in the words of James, been "set on fire by Hell", and caused great destruction over many years of our marriage. I know all the tongue's tricks for escaping the bridle from personal experience. The times are beyond counting where I have said something that I had not intended to be destructive, yet it has caused great hurt. I have then followed the expression of hurt with a pained effort at self-justification, and the die would be cast for the next three or four hours – quite frequently into the early hours of the morning, so carrying its ravages into the next day in tiredness as well as emotional damage. And I can safely say that every time this has happened, I have eventually come to see a motive behind those "harmless" – but idle – words that were in some way corrupt. It may have been critical, it may have been self-glorifying or self-justifying, it may have been selfishly attention-seeking: what they all had in common was that they did *not* "impart grace". Instead of edifying, they destroyed.

As Jesus tells us, the mouth speaks "out of the abundance (*perisseuma*) of the heart" (Matt. 12:34). The Greek root word here means to super-abound or overflow: think of water overflowing from a full bath or sink. Even though God gave us a new heart when we were born again, the old one still beats in all of us; and damage is done when it overflows. The heart of the old man looks to self; the heart of the new man looks to Jesus. When destructive words are spoken it is always because at some level the desires or the security of the self – the old man – are feeling threatened, whereas when we love we are obeying "the whole of the law". To ensure, then, that "no corrupt word" comes from our lips, is to ensure that we are always looking to Jesus and that we are always motivated by love. It means checking that the hidden intentions of our hearts are pure, and that we are not about to "overflow" out of a place that, under the light of the Holy Spirit, is far less innocent than it seemed when those idle words popped into our minds. Always very direct, James tells us that we must "Speak . . . as those who are judged by the law of liberty" (Jas. 2:12). And if, as the apostle Peter makes clear in his first epistle, our enemy the devil is always on the prowl and seeking to devour us, we don't want to help him out by handing him the ammunition of our unchecked words.

Will we always succeed? No. But grace is there for us every time we fail, so we keep aiming for that goal. In Psalm 73, the writer tells of his emotions towards the prosperity of the wicked, and how it was only when he came into the Temple one day that he saw the bitterness that had started to infect his heart. In the light of this revelation, "Why should I bother?" becomes "Lord, You're all I've got!" Complaint died on his lips, and the words that were uttered were words of praise and worship. David asks God to search his heart, to see if there are any wicked ways in him. The best way to control our tongue and stay victorious in the battle of our lives is to let the Holy Spirit search our hearts in the peace of His presence.

The seesaw

There is one more aspect of this "idle overflow of the heart" that I can comment on from a perspective of personal experience –

one where I have to say with Paul, even after thirty-five years of walking in salvation, that "I have not already attained, but I press on toward the goal". I was brought up in a culture of blame. If something went wrong in our family, a finger was pointed. If an inexplicable accident had occurred – I recall my father discovering a snapped branch on one of his garden shrubs – it had been "done deliberately". Arguments raged about who was "in the wrong". Conversation at the dinner-table often revolved around who was "to blame" for the ills of society. How different from the culture of Heaven! Our heavenly Father so loved the world that He gave His only Son to die on a cross, so that the finger of blame could be pointed, once and for all eternity, to Jesus. In his letter to the Philippians, Paul exhorts the Church:

> "Do everything without grumbling or arguing, so that you may become blameless and pure, 'children of God without fault in a warped and crooked generation.' Then you will shine among them like stars in the sky as you hold firmly to the word of life."

(Phil. 2:14-16 NIV)

There is a connection between a negative overflow of idle words – grumbling, arguing – and the carrying of blame. Jesus took all our guilt and all our shame to the cross. He nailed it there, once and for all. Never should a Christian carry blame. The exchange for sin and repentance is grace and forgiveness, not the burden of blame. Bickering and arguing is often motivated by a voice that says, "It's not my fault! Why should I get the blame?" – yet here the Holy Spirit tells us that we actually draw blame onto ourselves (thus denying the cross) by giving expression to that thought. How do we avoid carrying blame? By not arguing about whether or not we should be blamed – by not even thinking about it. Paul is specific: it is by achieving this state of living without that cross-denying sense of blame that we are able to let the light of Christ shine through us and, as we have shown in chapter seven, "hold firmly to the word of life".

So if we don't overflow with idle words, what do we overflow with? Colossians 2:6-7 gives us the answer:

> "As you therefore have received Christ Jesus the Lord, so walk in Him, rooted and built up in Him and established in the faith, as you have been taught, abounding in it with thanksgiving."

We find the same Greek root here again: *perisseuō*. Paul uses this word a lot: we find it no less than 16 times in his epistles. In fact it is a key word in the expression of one of Paul's great themes, spelled out no more clearly than in Romans 5:20: "where sin abounded, grace abounded much more". Because of the abundance of grace that God has caused to overflow into our lives, love, thanksgiving and good works will pour out. "For all things are for your sakes, that grace, having spread through the many, may cause thanksgiving to abound to the glory of God"

(2 Cor. 4:15).

Probably all of us who have taken children to a playground have put a small person on a seesaw (in the USA, probably a teeter-totter) and sat with a bump on the other end. We have probably pretended to get off and caused a squeal of protest. In Christ, we are the child on a seesaw of cosmic proportions, but it is one that will never move or bump: Jesus is sitting on the one end, carrying the weight of all our sin and shame; while we are on the other, lifted into heavenly places. Jesus is never going to get off; we are never going to drop down. In this place, the overflow of my heart can only be one thing: not complaint or argument about what man might do, or say, or think about me, but thanksgiving for what Christ has done.

If we cannot control our tongues, James tells us, our religion is "useless" – just as prophecy or faith, or any other spiritual gifting without love, is worthless and empty and will avail nothing (1 Cor. 13). Only love – God's love, poured into our hearts by the Holy Spirit – can control the tongue. When Jesus stood in the Temple and spoke of the Rivers of living water that would pour out of the spirit-filled Church, He was not just referring to an occasional utterance in tongues; He was talking about the overflow of a life abounding in the grace of God. When we, as warriors of this grace, drink from our cupped hands, there is no place for idle words.

Bible references

Acts 2:4

Psalm 19:14

Matthew 12:36-37

Proverbs 18:21

Romans 7:24-25

2 Corinthians 10:5

Proverbs 15:4

Proverbs 13:3

Joshua 6:1-27

Matthew 11:12

Mark 8:24

Matthew 17:21

Ephesians 4:29

1 Corinthians 1:27

2 Corinthians 12:9

Matthew 12:34

James 2:12

Psalm 73

Philippians 2:14-16

Colossians 2:6-7

Romans 5:20

2 Corinthians 4:15

1 Corinthians 13

Chapter Ten
Provisions: The Armour of God

Gideon did not lead his army into battle without equipment and provisions. God has provided spiritual weapons – the word of God and the gifts of the Holy Spirit – along with armour for our daily warfare: we cannot fight without them. The Ephesians 6 armour of God is not ours to put on, but His, and we wear it when we are clothed in Christ.

At last, Gideon has picked his team – or, rather, God has picked his team for him. Verse 8 says this:

"So the people took provisions and their trumpets in their hands. And he sent away all *the rest of* Israel, every man to his tent, and retained those three hundred men. Now the camp of Midian was below him in the valley."

(Judg. 7:8)

It was night time; the camp of Midian was amassed below him in the valley. What do we do when darkness is on us, and the enemy is swarming all around? This verse can easily be glossed over as just a link in the narrative of supernatural or extraordinary events that is the story of Gideon, but in it we find three important principles: the people took provisions, they took trumpets, and the camp of Midian was below them. Let's unpack them one at a time, remembering always the context, because it is worth repeating – darkness is upon us (we know this from verse 9, where the account refers to "the same night"), and the enemy is all around.

First point: they took provisions. They weren't about to go home for dinner, nor did they just have the next day's packed lunch in a rucksack: they had all the sustenance that they expected to need for the duration of the battle. What about us? Do we go into battle stocked up with all the provision we need? We know from the story of Abraham and Isaac that our heavenly Father is Jehovah Jireh – The Lord shall Provide. We know from the letter to the Philippians that this Jehovah Jireh will supply "all your need according to His riches in glory by Christ Jesus" (Phil. 4:19). Most of us can find, or quote, many verses that confirm the truth of God's abundant providence. They build our faith for God's material provision in our lives; they reassure us of our Kingdom inheritance as adopted sons of God. Yet how often do we lay hold of the double-sided truth that a) the advancement of the Kingdom, to which all of us are called, puts us, *ipso facto*, on a war footing; and therefore that b) Jehovah Jireh will provide – has already provided – everything we need for success? Paul writes (2 Cor. 10:4): "For the *weapons* of our warfare are not *carnal*, but mighty in God for pulling down *strongholds." God has provided spiritual weapons, mighty ones, for the defeat of our spiritual enemy. We find our supply in 1 Corinthians 12, beginning* "Now concerning spiritual *gifts,* brethren, I do not want you to be ignorant . . ." (v.1).

The gifts, or the "manifestation of the Spirit" (v.7) are listed in the following order: word of wisdom, word of knowledge, faith, healings, miracles, prophecy, discerning of spirits, tongues and interpretation of tongues. I believe that these gifts are an essential part of God's provision for our battles. There can often be a strange contradiction at work in the area of provision and battlegrounds, which I would say is a deception of the enemy. As a rule, we expect to use – or witness someone else using – the gifts of the Spirit within a church congregation. On the other hand, it is likely that we see church as a place of respite from the battle: that is something that rages in the world's settings, in the workplace or even at home. Yet if we think that there are no spiritual powers of darkness at work when we gather together to worship we are deceiving ourselves, and if we think that the Holy Spirit only wants to manifest Jesus on a Sunday morning when the worship group are playing we have completely missed the point.

In the Acts 2 scheme of things as to how revelation is received, I would say that I have for some years come into the "dreamer of dreams" category. Just before I awoke the morning after writing the paragraph above, I had the following dream. Whether this was God-given, or just the workings of my subconscious mind on a topic of the previous day, is something I will never know until the day when I "know all things"; however, it does communicate a powerful and relevant message. The details, as I remember them, are as follows.

I was taking part in a live stand-up comedy show, and was due to go onstage at 9.00 p.m. I was with a group of people, one of whom was also due to perform. The time was 8.45. I suddenly realised that a) I hadn't got any clothes ready, and b) I was relying on my native ability as a raconteur and wit, and hadn't got anything specifically prepared. My performance was due to last one hour. I had a trunk of clothes and a wardrobe. There was a suit and white dress-shirt in the wardrobe; the trunk was full of casual clothes. The other performer said I should go onstage dressed casually, but everything in the wardrobe was extremely crumpled. And how could I find time for ironing? I still had to write my script, and now it was 8.50 and I had ten minutes left. I tried on the white shirt from the wardrobe, despite my friend's advice, and immediately felt comfortable: this is what I should wear. Yet there was a problem here as well: there was an ornate collection of gold studs round the collar, which prevented me from doing it up or putting on the bow tie that went with it. I was very glad to open my eyes and find myself in bed . . .

 God has purposed that "the manifold wisdom of God might be made known by the church to the principalities and powers in the heavenly places" (Eph. 3:10). In the same way as I was about to go out onstage in my dream, we are put on display to be a demonstration of God's wisdom in heavenly places. In the spiritual dimension, God has decreed that our battle should be fought on a public stage so that His wisdom, the victory at Calvary, is spelled out to the principalities and powers in the heavenly audience. I wasn't unprepared in my dream because I had been delayed in any way; I was unprepared, woefully so, because I had been lazy and presumptuous, imagining that all I had to do was to go out and just be myself, and in doing so would have the audience in thrall for the next 60 minutes.

To start with, I didn't even have the script. To recall Judges 7:8, I had no provisions in my hands. Primarily, our script is the word of God, the "sword of the Spirit". This must be one of the most frequently quoted phrases in the Bible, and because of its familiarity it can be easy to gloss over. "Yes, I know, His word is Spirit and life, Jesus said so, let's move on . . ." But the point is this: God's words, when *they were spoken by Jesus*, were Spirit and life.

 "It is the Spirit who gives life; the flesh profits nothing. The words that I speak to you are spirit, and *they* are life."

(John 6:63)

This doesn't mean that every time we speak God's words they are Spirit and life. The devil can quote scripture: he did when he tempted Jesus, and he still does today. We can't just pick up our Bibles and claim to be holding the sword of the Spirit. We only have the sword of the Spirit in our hands when Jesus, by the Holy Spirit in us, is speaking the words.

We read at the end of the gospel of Mark that God would confirm His word by "signs and wonders following". One man whose ministry has been followed by more signs and wonders than most people who have lived on this planet is Smith Wigglesworth, who raised more people from the dead than we read about in the whole of the New Testament – a true "greater things than these will you do" disciple of Jesus; a man whom – if God himself so confirms his words – we should be taking seriously. This is what he says:

"The gift of intercession, the gift of laying hands on the sick, the gift of prophecy, the gift of the word of wisdom, the gift of the word of knowledge, the gift of discerning spirits, the gift of tongues, the gift of interpretation – all these are included in this one verse: *"Now concerning spiritual gifts, brethren, I do not want you to be ignorant"* (1 Cor. 12:1). So I implore you to think seriously in your heart – because you need to be in the world but not of it – that you need to be a personal manifestation of the living Christ. Just as Jesus walked about the earth, you have to walk about as a child of God, with power and manifestation."

(From *Smith Wigglesworth on Spiritual Gifts,* Whitaker House, 1998)

The sword of the Spirit, with which we must be equipped and which God has provided, is the word of God *that is wielded by the Holy Spirit,* as we speak His truth *and* manifest His presence and power. This is one key element of the provision that God has made available for us so that we are prepared for battle. In focusing on this we cannot ignore the rest of the Ephesians 6 armour of God – the helmet of salvation, the breastplate of righteousness, the shield of faith, the belt of truth, the shoes of the gospel of peace: knowing that God has given us these, understanding what they are, putting them on and making sure they fit, is all part of "knowing the script". Without this provision we go out onto that stage defenceless and unprepared, and all we witness to is our religion.

Battle garb

The other detail of the dream was the question of clothing. What should I wear? Everything in the trunk was creased and rumpled, and I had no time for ironing. In fact there would have been no point, because I can provide nothing of my own. All my righteousness was as filthy rags, and there they were, lying in a heap in the trunk. We cannot prepare ourselves for the battle, other than by spending time taking hold of what God has already prepared for us. In my dream, I knew that only one thing was appropriate: it was the white shirt hanging in the wardrobe. It fitted perfectly, and indeed there was nothing else.

In our Christian lives, this is the battle garb: "And the armies in heaven, clothed in fine linen, white and clean, followed Him on white horses" (Rev. 19:14).

In the third chapter of Romans, Paul shows how the righteousness of God, through faith in Christ, is demonstrated "through . . . all and on all who believe" (Rom. 3:22). The "breastplate of righteousness" is an essential part of the armour of God described in Ephesians 6. This same breastplate – the one worn with the "helmet the hope of salvation" – is described to the Thessalonians as "the breastplate of faith and love" (1 Thess. 5:8 ESV). Righteousness, faith and love are all beaten together into this one breastplate in Galatians 5:5-6:

> "For we through the Spirit eagerly wait for the hope of righteousness by faith. For in Christ Jesus neither circumcision nor uncircumcision avails anything, but faith working through love."

Here then is the white shirt of my dream without which I could not go onstage, the white linen of the armies of Heaven, the wedding gown of the parable (Matt. 22) without which we cannot enter the banquet of the Kingdom of God: it is the righteousness of God which is ours through faith in Christ, demonstrated through the love God has put into our hearts. But there was a final twist to my dream: although I had clearly got the right shirt available, I could not wear it. There were various gold studs and embellishments on the collar, which prevented me from putting on a bow tie and doing it up. Our robe of righteousness has no place for attention-seeking embellishment. There was nothing else in the cupboard, and my time was up: I was not going to be ready to go onstage. Panicking, I woke up.

We cannot know "the day or the hour" of the culmination of God's purposes on earth and the return of Christ, but we do know that we must be ready, with our lamps filled and trimmed, as the parable of the ten virgins illustrates. Some observers would say that many end-time prophecies are being or already have been fulfilled, and that the time when the Church is really thrust into end-time battle stations is nearly upon us. In our cosseted Western lives our condition is almost dreamlike: with bank loans and credit cards, who needs faith for God's supply? With drugstores and doctors, who needs miracles of healing? We have Google: who needs words of wisdom? We see TV documentaries: who needs to see the spirit realm? Ask those who were Christians in China in the 1980s. Ask the Christians in North Korea. Ask the brothers in Africa, where sorcerers call down lightning on Christian meetings. Ask those who have seen friends and family beheaded by Islamic State jihadists. Banks can fail, medicines can run out, and electricity can be cut off. We must wake up to the reality of the spiritual battle around us: we need to be standing in the purposes of God.

And He has provided His righteousness: it is perfect and complete; we cannot add to it with our talents, our knowledge or our religion. Psalm 85:13 tells us: "Righteousness will go before Him, and shall make His footsteps *our* pathway."

We cannot walk in His footsteps unless we are wearing His breastplate. If we go into battle without it, we will be mown down. If we think we've got it right, we haven't: we're em-bellishingthe God-given garment of righteousness and making it unwearable. Galatians 3:2 again: we are beginning in the Spirit, and then trying to make ourselves perfect in the flesh.

I cannot speak for others, but I know that I have always tended to personalise the rest of the armour of God when reading Ephesians 6. I have listened to, or read, teaching that paints a picture of Paul in his prison cell, looking at a Roman soldier on guard duty and likening the various aspects of our Christian walk with the armour he can see. We imagine Paul pondering on how the knowledge of our salvation is like a helmet that keeps our thinking on a godly track. We think of our faith extinguishing fiery darts of doubt and fear. We buckle our belt, keeping all our garments in place as we declare the truths of the word of God. Our faith, our helmet, our belt and so on – not so much the armour of God, but the armour of godliness.

But Paul's pen is not the only one that the Holy Spirit used to tell us about His armour. Hundreds of years before Paul was writing to the Ephesians, Isaiah wrote prophetically of Jesus:

"He saw that *there was* no man,
And wondered that *there was* no intercessor;
Therefore His own arm brought salvation for Him;
And His own righteousness, it sustained Him,
For He put on righteousness as a breastplate,
And a helmet of salvation on His head."

(Isa. 59:16-17)

The helmet of salvation

We have already explored how we cannot wear our own righteousness, or do anything to add to what the Lord has provided; and we have seen that it is the Spirit, not us, who wields the sword of God's word. It is clear from these verses that the helmet, too, belongs to the Lord Jesus. We do not wear "our" helmet of salvation: we wear His. Is this not a different level? The strength and the very existence of the helmet we wear does not depend on the level of our certainty, our detailed knowledge of the Scriptures or our understanding of reformist theology. It is not just a symbol that came to Paul to illustrate the condition of our renewed mind: the helmet of salvation is what Jesus wore when God's "own arm brought salvation for Him". It's His helmet that He has given to us. As we face the enemy, the protection over our thought-life is the same as Jesus was wearing when He won the victory at Calvary. He removes it from His head and offers it to us, saying, "Here you are. This is for you." It isn't going to fail.

The shield of faith

God's righteousness is our breastplate. The Holy Spirit wields His sword, the word of God. We wear the Lord's helmet on our heads. The faith, our shield, is also not our own. The Greek used for Jesus's words in Mark 11:22, "Have faith in God", is better rendered as "Have the faith of God". Ephesians 2:8 tells us: "For by grace you have been saved through faith, and that not of yourselves; *it is* the gift of God." The faith that led us to salvation comes from God. We do not create faith in our minds: all faith is God given. We learn in Romans 12:3 that "God has dealt to each one a measure of faith". When Jesus tells us to "have faith in God" He is telling us that God is giving us a measure of His faith – the faith that called the universe into being at the speaking of His creative word; "the evidence of things not seen" (Heb. 11:1). This shield of faith, which extinguishes the fiery darts of doubt ("Did God say . . . ?) and fear, tells us that God's word is truth and life. Like the helmet of salvation, the shield of faith is fashioned entirely by God: it is made of the very fabric of God's creative power (the faith of God), and it is provided for us as a gift. We cannot go into battle without it.

The belt of truth

The item that "girds up our loins", ready for action, is one thing that our post-modern world says does not exist: absolute truth. Paul writes to Timothy: "Now the Spirit expressly says that in latter times some will depart from the faith, giving heed to deceiving spirits and doctrines of demons . . ." (1 Tim. 4:1). Later in the same letter he says: "Teach these truths, Timothy, and encourage everyone to obey them . . . they are the sound, wholesome teachings of the Lord Jesus Christ, and are the foundation for a godly life (1 Tim. 6:2-3 TLB). He tells the Galatians: "But even if we, or an angel from heaven, preach any other gospel to you than what we have preached to you, let him be accursed" (Gal. 1:8). This gospel of the grace of God through Jesus Christ is outrageous; it is astonishing; but it is clear and straightforward: God really did so love the world "that He gave His only begotten Son, that whoever believes in Him should not perish but have everlasting life" (John 3:16). We buckle "these truths" round our waists and we run with them in place, shod with the message of reconciliation that God has given us – "the shoes of the gospel of peace" – His peace (John 14:27), not peace as the world gives.

The point is this: all of the items in our armoury are not only God-given; they partake of the actual nature of God. Psalm 93:1 says, "The LORD is clothed, He has girded Himself with strength." The armour that He is wearing is the armour that we put on. This is the Armour of God.

So like Gideon's men, we take our provisions. We do not go into battle empty handed, but we take all the divine amour and every spiritual weapon that God has made available. We can ask for spiritual gifts like words of knowledge or gifts of healing, and by faith we can "take them in our hands", believing that they will manifest when they are needed. We know that the righteousness of God is ours by faith in Christ, and we can go out and love our enemies wearing that righteousness as our breastplate, knowing that we have been freely forgiven and justified, and that nothing can separate us from the love of God which is ours in Christ. We equip ourselves with the word of God, and we allow the Holy Spirit to wield it. We take the helmet and the shield that He has fashioned and provided, clasp the belt of His truth round our waists and prepare ourselves to walk in His peace. Thus clothed in God's strength, we look down onto the Midianites below us in the valley, and we pick up our trumpets.

Bible references

Judges 7:8

Philippians 4:19

2 Corinthians 10:4

1 Corinthians 12:1

Ephesians 3:10

John 6:63

Revelation 19:14

Romans 3:24

1 Thessalonians 5:8

Galatians 5:5-6

Psalm 85:13

Galatians 3:2

Isaiah 59:16-17

Mark11:22

Ephesians 2:8

Romans 12:3
Hebrews 11:1
1 Timothy 4:1; 6:2-3
Galatians 1:8
John 3:16; 14:27
Psalm 93:1

Chapter Eleven
Position and Praise

As Gideon looked down on the enemy, so do we from our position raised up in Christ. Whatever our circumstances, God is forever worthy of our praise; and with it we can "awaken the dawn" when darkness seems to descend on our lives. In doing so we can see our battle from the heavenly perspective.

Where do we see the enemy? Gideon saw him "below him in the valley". They may have been massed in all directions, but they were below. By contrast, the Holy Spirit repeatedly affirms through scripture that our position is above. John the Baptist says of Jesus: "The one who comes from above is above all" (John 3:31 NIV). Paul goes into greater detail: when God Raised Jesus from the dead, He "seated *Him* at His right hand in the heavenly *places,* far above all principality and power and might and dominion, and every name that is named, not only in this age but also in that which is to come" (Eph. 1:20-21). If we are "in Christ", we are also in His position. As Gideon looked down on the Midianites in the valley, we, from the place where we have been raised, look down on "all principality and power and might and dominion".

Before he died, Moses gave a blessing to each of the twelve tribes. Finally he blessed the whole of Israel with these words:

> "Happy are you, O Israel!
> Who is like you, a people saved by the LORD,
> The shield of your help
> And the sword of your majesty!
> Your enemies shall submit to you
> And you shall tread down their high places."

(Deut. 33:29)

The High Places were considered to be areas of spiritual dominion. Idols were set up and altars built on them. Not only were they sites of Canaanite pagan worship but they were visited by Samuel (1 Sam. 7:16). Solomon lost the Kingdom because he worshipped with his foreign wives at idolatrous high places that he established for them outside Jerusalem, and the practice of worshipping Baal and other idols continued at various high places throughout the infidelity of Israel and Judah. God, who met with Moses on a mountaintop, permitted one High Place only, and that was the Temple at Jerusalem; and now Jesus is raised to the "highest place of all", where, in Him, amazingly, outrageously, we are also seated (Eph. 1:21; 2:6).

LOOK UP- NOT DOWN:

So as Gideon looked down on the enemy camp, so too do we – but from a far greater height. Whatever our battle, we have been given dominion in Christ. From our position of victory, we can choose: we either look down at the enemy massed against us, or we can look up and see limitless power. When Jesus, the one who was and is above all, blessed the loaves and fishes so that they would feed 5,000 people, he didn't look down at all the hungry people; he "looked up to Heaven" first. He knew His Father's provision would meet the need. Like Elisha (2 Kgs 6:15-16), who asked God to open the eyes of his servant to see the armies of Heaven ranged against their enemy, we see that those who are with us are immeasurably greater than the one who is against us; and that the word of God given to us in Isaiah 54:17 is true for our own lives.

THOSE WHO KEPT THEIR EYE's FIXED N' FOCUSED

"No weapon formed against you shall prosper,   ON JESUS
And every tongue which rises against you in judgement
You shall condemn.

This is the heritage of the servants of the Lord,
And their righteousness is from Me,
Says the Lord."

The storm and the stance of faith

We are given a graphic lesson of our battle position in the gospel account of Peter in the storm on the lake. The story is usually picked up when the disciples are already in the boat, but actually it begins much earlier, at the beginning of Matthew 14, where it is reported that Herod first heard about Jesus. The Kingdom of God is advancing; the word is being preached and people are being healed and delivered. Satan is rattled. Through his own servants, Herod, Salome and her daughter, he launches a counter-attack, and has John the Baptist beheaded. When Jesus hears that His cousin has been killed He knows He must stop everything and seek His Father, so He procures a boat to go off by himself to pray (v.13). However, it wasn't going to be that simple – He was tracked down by 5,000 people who wanted His time to start with, and then were in need of food. What would we do, faced with 5,000 needy, hungry people when all we want is a quiet time with Father? But – because He is the King – Jesus sought the Kingdom. The obstacle to His prayer time became an opportunity to reveal God's provision, and at the same time to demonstrate to His followers (that includes us) the sovereign power of His command "You give them something to eat".

Having shown them (and us) the truth behind his mother's words at the wedding in Cana – "Whatever He says to you, [*you can*] do it" – He tells His disciples to take the boat and go ahead of Him to Gennasaret, and sends the crowds away. They are healed, taught and provided for; He carries on and spends time with Father as He had planned, and the disciples are heading over the water under His command to continue the work of the Kingdom on the other side of the lake.

Satan sees that his plan is failing – Jesus hasn't been warned or put off; in fact the opposite has happened – and His followers are heading for the next destination. But – could this be an opportunity to hinder the work? They are travelling alone, without their master. A storm – that should do the trick. We know what happens next. This is a well-known and much interpreted story: we hear and read about the storms of life that inevitably come our way, and how to deal with them – all of which is good, sound teaching. But personally I think – as I have already intimated – that this storm didn't just blow up on the lake: I think Satan sent it as a direct attack on the work of the Kingdom. There are reliable accounts from the mission field of witch doctors in Africa calling down storms on gospel meetings – Mahesh Chavda and Reinhart Bonnke, for example, both tell of such events – so if the powers of darkness today can raise a supernatural storm at the bidding of a witch doctor; how much more are they likely to launch a similar attack on the contemporary disciples of Jesus?

The point is this: the disciples were going about the business of the Kingdom, and the wind was against them. We have to know that the wind will always be against us when we go about the business of the Kingdom. The problem on this occasion was that the disciples "hadn't understood about the loaves" (Mark 6:52): they hadn't understood that they had fed the 5,000 because Jesus had told them to, so they didn't realise that they were going to cross the lake because Jesus had told them to. When Jesus called out to them on the water, Peter – probably under the inspiration of the Holy Spirit – briefly caught a glimpse of the power of the Lord's word when he said (Matt.14:28), "Lord, if it is You, command me to come to You on the water." So when Jesus said, "Come," Peter walked. Peter was walking on the word, not on the water: Satan's storm was below him, and he was looking above the waves, into the face of Jesus. Until he noticed the wind.

Suddenly Peter "saw that the wind was boisterous [and] was afraid" (v.30). Do you ever wonder how many steps Peter had taken before he noticed the wind? It isn't as if the wind had just started blowing at that moment. But while Peter was walking on the word "Come", the storm couldn't touch him. No weapon formed against him could prosper. But something took his eyes off the face of Jesus: Peter immediately forgot the upholding power of the word he had been given, and fear jumped in. Instead of being above the enemy's waves, they began to get on top of him. Fortunately when we start sinking like this we can always cry out to Jesus, and He will reach out His hand like He did to Peter. But He will say to us what He said to Peter: "Ye of little faith. Why did you doubt?"

Poor Peter! we might think. Here is the guy who had the courage to step out of the boat, who actually WALKED ON THE WATER

IN THE STORM, for crying out loud; and Jesus tells him off? Where's the "Well done for getting this far, Peter"?

We must leave aside our human thinking here. We must leave aside the voice of our education system and our parenting culture that says "effort must be rewarded". There is no need for this in our relationship with the King: we have already been accepted by Him, lifted by Him, and seated with Him in heavenly places. We don't need an effort grade. In fact we can achieve nothing in the Kingdom of God by our own efforts, so a pat on the back for trying is actually the last thing we need. If we look at the waves instead of Him; if we try and walk on the water instead of on the word, we are looking down instead of looking up, and we are losing our position of victory. "Ye of little faith, why did you doubt?" isn't a telling off; it is a telling of truth. If we are doubting, we need to let Him show us the answer to His question, so that we can learn to walk fearlessly on His word.

The response of praise

As there is only one position of faith, so there is only one response appropriate for our hearts: the response of praise. Taking hold of their provisions and their trumpets, Gideon and his men looked down on the Midianite camp. Taking hold of all that God has provided for us, we stand in our position of victory, and we praise the Lord.

Many and various are the teachings on the power of praise. The instruction from Psalm 150:6 is unequivocal: "Let everything that

has breath praise the LORD", as is the injunction in 1 Thessalonians
5:18 – "in everything give thanks; for this is the will of God in
Christ Jesus for you" and David's assertion in Psalm 34:1 – "I will
bless the LORD at all times; His praise shall continually be in my
mouth."

Everything? At all times? Continually? Why?

I was listening to a classical music station in the car when a
recording of a well-known soprano came on the air singing the
hymn "Abide With Me". One couplet seemed to reach out and
take hold of me:

> "Change and decay in all around I see;
> Oh Thou who changest not, abide with me."

At that moment, driving along a main road in Staffordshire, I can
only say that I had a fresh revelation of the eternal, unchanging
nature of our God. For the next two days if was on my mind
constantly: God's faithfulness, His love, His mercy, are from
everlasting and will endure forever. His grace is unstoppable.
His glory will fill the earth because it has to – nothing can stand
in the way. Nothing can possibly separate us from the love of
God which is ours in Christ Jesus – nothing could be powerful
enough to be an obstacle. By contrast, as the psalmist says, we
are dust, we are grass. All our anxieties, all our fears, everything
that brings us grief, is somehow connected to the fact that our
flesh is not eternal; our comfort, our pleasure, our security, our
life itself – all is subject to change and decay and potential loss.

Happiness in a relationship can be destroyed in a moment by a thoughtless word or action. Illness, financial ruin, accidents, natural disaster, crime – all can strike in an instant and take away what we value the most. The gift that God gives – His Kingdom, His life – has none of these so when the time announced by the book of Revelation finally comes there will be no more death or crying or pain. And the Holy Spirit, the deposit of this Kingdom poured into our hearts now, has been given to us, bringing the presence, the love and the power of the eternal King Himself into our lives, today, on this transient Earth. Whatever changes are taking place around us, how can there be anything but praise in our hearts for the One who lives in us who is unchanging, and by whose grace our own perishable nature will finally "put on incorruption" (1 Cor. 15:54)?

Clapping away the crows

Psalm 108 teaches us the position of praise. David writes (vs.1):

"O God, my heart is steadfast; I will sing and give praise, even with my glory."

The Hebrew for "steadfast" is a root word, meaning fixed or established. It is used throughout the Old Testament for the eternal works of God's hands: Proverbs 3:19 tells us how God established the heavens by understanding; the song of Moses tells us of the sanctuary which God has established (Exod. 15:17). Our position in Christ is, equally, the work of God's hands. He has lifted us to be with Him in these same heavenly places which He has established, and He planned this work before the beginning of time: Heaven was created to be shared with the redeemed. David has caught this revelation prophetically: he may see nothing but darkness all around, but he knows his position; he knows that when he commands his lute and harp to awake (v.2), it is he who will awaken the dawn. Are our instruments of praise asleep? Or are our hearts steadfast because we know where we are seated, and our eyes are on the greatness of our Lord who lifted us to that place?

David writes (vs.3-4)

> "I will sing praises to You among the nations,
> For Your mercy *is* great above the heavens,
> And Your truth *reaches* to the clouds."

It is a truism to say that we cannot measure or quantify God. But while we know that in the Lord Jesus He touches us at the deepest human level, we need to hold this in tension with the truth that the same person is the one who spoke to Job out of the whirlwind (Job 38:1), and the description of whom was so beyond the reach of Ezekiel that he could get no nearer than a faltering "appearance of the likeness of the glory of the LORD" (Ezek. 1:28).

The following insight was shared prophetically by a member of Wildwood Church recently. I believe it was given to us by the Holy Spirit. The following words are my attempt at accurately conveying what was shared:

"We see a flower as a flower. An insect will perceive that flower very differently; a different insect will perceive it differently again, and every animal likewise, so that one flower becomes a universe of different perceptions in different hues and scents, from all parts of every relevant spectrum: the sum of every impression received by every creature encountering that flower. We, God's children, are fearfully and wonderfully made. While we see each other through our human eyes, God sees every detail of every aspect of who we are that He has created – the whole universe of who we are, not the little three-dimensional image that we have of ourselves and each other. And similarly the full reality of the nature of God explodes beyond our three-dimensional thinking, to the extent that anything that even comes close to an approximation of the truth will bring us trembling to our knees. And just as this is the inexpressible extent of His majesty and glory, so it is the depth and passion of the love that went to Calvary for our sins."

So True

This, indeed, is the mercy that is "great above the heavens", the truth that "reaches to the clouds", the One who, from everlasting to everlasting, is worthy of our praise.

Finally, in vs.5-6, David continues:

"Be exalted, O God, above the heavens,
And Your glory above all the earth;
That Your beloved may be delivered,
Save *with* Your right hand, and hear me."

146

God is who He is: "I am that I am". He does not depend on our praise to be exalted. But it is out of his circumstances that David is singing God's praises. God is exalted above all the Earth, but when our praise brings our own situations into line with His dominion the door for our deliverance is thrown open. This is illustrated quite literally in Acts 16:16-30, in the story of Paul and Silas in prison: as they praised God, exalting Him over their imprisonment, the prison doors were thrown open. We have no record of the details of their worship time, but it is not beyond the realms of possibility that Paul and Silas were declaring God's praises in the words of the psalm quoted above. Paul writes: "For the trumpet will sound, and the dead will be raised incorruptible, and we shall be changed" (1 Cor. 15:52). When we sound the trumpet of praise, not only are we announcing this incorruptible Kingdom to ourselves ("Bless the LORD, O my soul, and forget not all His benefits" – Ps. 103:2), but to the principalities and powers in the spiritual realms.

From my study window I look out across our garden onto the woodlands of Cannock Chase. It is beautiful; it is tranquil. Nonetheless, we live in a fallen world, and for a couple of weeks in the summer, when the younger generation from the neighbourhood rookery have flown the nest but are still with the colony, they descend on a tree at the end of our garden, and even on the roof above our bedroom, and have loud, raucous conversations at five o'clock in the morning. I am a bird-lover, but my love for birds does not extend to rooks and crows, who, as well as waking me up at dawn, raid nests and kill baby birds. In much literature, and also in my own imagination, crows symbolise death, darkness and the demonic. For many mornings I awoke much earlier than intended, thanks to their alarm call; then one morning, I remembered that these birds of darkness are also great cowards: the slightest disturbance will drive them away. I opened the window and clapped my hands; about twenty-five crows spread their wings as one and flew away, cawing, into the woods. Not long afterwards, I went back to sleep.

There will be times when the crows descend on our lives. But it is given to us, not to the darkness surrounding our circumstances, to "awaken the dawn". Like Gideon looking down on the enemy, we need to remember to clap away the crows.

Bible references

John 3:31
Ephesians 1:20-21
Deuteronomy 33:29
Ephesians 1:21
Ephesians 2:6
2 Kings 6:15-16
Isaiah 54:17
Matthew 14:13,28,30
Mark 6:52
Matthew 14:28,30
Psalm 150:6
1 Thessalonians 5:18
Psalm 34:1

1 Corinthians 15:54

Psalm 108:1-6

Ezekiel 1:28

1 Corinthians 15:52

Psalm 103:2

Chapter Twelve
Moving into the Victory

God tells Gideon to "arise", as He has delivered the Midianites into his hand. To move into victory, we first need to "Arise" – which is a stance that runs counter to our couch-potato culture. Even though we have the victory, we still have to fight the battles. Jesus asks us to reach by faith into the provision that He has delivered at the cross.

J udges 7:9 continues: "It happened on the same night that the LORD said to him, 'Arise, go down against the camp, for I have delivered it into your hand.'"

Arise. We often quote, or hear quoted, the glorious verses from Isaiah 60, beginning "Arise, shine, for your light has come!" But have we ever considered how contrary this word is to the spirit of our age, especially in the West? A multi-billion dollar industry exists to achieve a single purpose: the removal, or at least the minimising, of the need to arise. Instead of walking, we drive; instead of getting up to change TV channels, we press a button on the remote; we cover our gardens with paving slabs to eliminate the exertion of cultivating flower beds and pulling up weeds. More and more industrial processes are carried out remotely, by an operator sitting at a computer. Unless we are intentional about exercise, many of us can so easily get into our cars in the morning, drive to work, sit at a desk all day, drive home again, eat food that has been pre-prepared, wash up with a dishwasher, spend the evening watching TV on the sofa, and go to bed. The new technology market is robotics: there are already robot vacuum cleaners, robot lawn mowers, and many others – all designed to relieve us of the need to "arise". Obesity is one of the biggest health problems in the UK and USA today; its friend laziness is becoming the lifestyle of much of the developed world.

The book of Proverbs has strong words to say about laziness, no more so than in chapter 26, where the progression moves from telling us in verse 12 that there is more hope for a fool than for a man who is "wise in his own eyes", to verse 16, where we read that the lazy man is "wiser in his own eyes than seven men who can answer sensibly". God sees laziness as one of the worst forms of folly – the foolishness of the person whose mind is closed to the wisdom of others, and above all to the wisdom of God. Effectively, what these scriptures tell us is that the lazier we become, the more we cut ourselves off from the mind of Christ. Against this background, the call to "Arise" is more than just a positive exhortation (Isa. 60:1), or an instruction to a group of warriors who were preparing for a night's rest: it is in itself a battle-cry; a call to shake ourselves free of a prevailing spirit of the age, to break the power of a demonic strategy designed to lead us sleepwalking into separation from God.

Knowing, therefore, that God has delivered the enemy into his hand, Gideon and his men go into battle. There is a tension here between knowing that the battle is won, and still having to fight it. The times in the history of Israel where God sovereignly destroyed the enemy (e.g. the deliverance from the Assyrians, 2 Kings 19; victory over Moab, 2 Kings 3) give us a glimpse of the overwhelming and absolute power of God over sin and death that was exercised at Calvary. In the eternal realms of the spirit, the battle is over, Christ is seated at the Father's right hand, and we are already seated there with Him. However, the story of Gideon gives us principles for the daily battle that we face while this dispensation of time still exists; while, under His reign, we engage with Him in the task of putting all His enemies under His feet (1 Cor. 15:25). We need to understand how to reconcile the two: how to arise, while remaining seated.

God's ready-mix

Early in 1997 Anne and I felt that God was calling us to move away from where we lived in Gloucestershire to be part of another work up in Staffordshire. The house was about to go on the market. It was a freezing spell in January. One morning, after a particularly cold, wet night, we awoke to find that a three- to four-metre length of our garden wall had collapsed. We lived in an old farm cottage, and this wall was built of stone, about four-feet high, double thickness. The rain had penetrated the wall during the night, had frozen and expanded and forced the stones apart, and now most of the outer skin of that length was lying in the wet grass. With a "For Sale" sign just about to go up by the gate, we had no choice but to try, like Nehemiah, to rebuild the wall.

At that time, neither of us were particularly fit: I had a back injury and could not lift; and Anne was in pain from the digestive tract disorder that I referred to earlier. However, I did possess some cement, a bucket and a bricklaying trowel, so I mixed a bucket of cement, Anne swallowed hard and carried it the twenty yards or so up the drive, we lifted the first stone back into place between us, and we proceeded to pour in the mortar mix. Because of all the gaps and crevices in the old wall and the way it was built, the bucketful was not even enough for the first stone.

We mixed another bucketful, but I was rapidly getting into a "What's the point?" mode: the job appeared totally impossible. By now it was also starting to rain. Anne said, "Lord, what we need is a lorry load of ready-mix" – and she was right: not even fifty buckets were going to be enough to fix that wall. I wanted to give up and go inside, but Anne was determined to keep going, even though the task appeared completely impossible. A few minutes later – we may have still been on the second bucket, or it may have been the third – I looked up, to see a tarmac lorry coming down the road. Anne said, "Look! There's our ready-mix". I said no – tarmac was for roads; it wouldn't be cement.

We lived opposite a school. To our surprise, the lorry turned into the school gates. Anne said, "Go on, go over and see if it's cement!" I was still convinced that it was tarmacadam, probably for the car park, and was (unbelievably!) still reluctant to go over and see. The book of Proverbs says that there is more hope for a fool than for a man who is wise in his own mind, and I certainly was that man. Fortunately Anne made sure I overcame my reluctance, and walked over to the school. The lorry was pumping out cement. It was, indeed, a lorry-load of ready-mix. I said to one of the men, "I don't suppose any of that is spare, is it?" He nodded over to an area of cement, four- or five-metres square, a little away from where the lorry was pumping. "Yes," he said, "that lot over there. Help yourself to as much as you want."

I ran in to get the wheelbarrow. Just then May, a friend from work, "just happened" to turn up. God had even provided extra man (or in this case, woman) power. I ran backwards and forwards refilling the barrow with cement, and, with May's help, as the rain fell and the evening gloom was gathering, we rebuilt the wall. We completed it in less than two hours.

We had experienced an astounding miracle of God's provision. But the point is this: if it hadn't been for Anne's willingness to "arise", we would have missed it. Without her determination to keep going, even though the resources to hand were hopelessly inadequate, we would have gone back into the house, we would never have seen the lorry, the cement would have stayed on the other side of the road, and our wall would not have been rebuilt. I drove past the house recently, on a visit to an old friend. After eighteen years, our wall was still standing. The section we had repaired looked stronger than the stones around it. It actually looked as though it will still be there when the rest of the wall has crumbled away, standing as a testimony to the work of God.

It's been delivered

There are no doubts in the word "delivered". A mail-order business depends on goods arriving in the hands of the person who has ordered them; safe delivery is essential to the success of the business. Mail and courier systems can fail at times, and parcels can occasionally go astray. Disputes may arise between a sender, who says that they have sent a parcel, and the consignee, who says that it hasn't arrived. A safeguard against such disputes is a "signed for" service, where someone signs for the parcel to say that it has arrived safely. If such a dispute arises and a signed-for service has been used, the sender can say with absolute certainty that the goods have been delivered.

The Hebrew word used in verse 9 has the same sense of certainty. Some of the associations are to give over, to entrust, to commit, to assign, to publish, to grant, to appoint. God is saying to Gideon, "There is no uncertainty here – the parcel has arrived, it's been signed for – go and get it."

God had delivered the enemy into Gideon's hands as definitely as He had delivered our cement. At the cross, He delivered salvation, healing, deliverance from evil and freedom from sin. He signed for the delivery in Isaiah 53:5:

"But He was wounded for our transgressions,
He was bruised for our iniquities;
The chastisement for our peace was upon Him,
And by His stripes we are healed."

But when the Tarmac lorry came down the road and even when it turned into the school gate opposite our house, what was my initial reaction? "That's not cement, and it's not for us." My flesh would have had me turn away. Anne's faith had me go over the road and look. Psalm 34:8 exhorts us to "Taste and see that the LORD is Good" – but it is only by faith, God's gift to us (Eph. 2:8), that we can go and taste. We need to cross the road. All God's provision was delivered at the cross, but we need to believe that it's everything we need, and we need to believe that it's for us. In our human thinking, even at our most religious, this is impossible: we need to cross the road and receive the delivery, our spiritual concrete, by faith.

Receiving the delivery

Jesus tells us (Mark 11:24): "Therefore I say to you, whatever things you ask when you pray, believe that you receive *them,* and you will have *them.*" The teaching is clear: what we have received in the dimension of the Spirit, we will experience in the dimension of the flesh. The Greek *lambano,* usually translated as "receive", is more definite and active than is conveyed by the English. It carries a sense of lay hold of, seize, grasp, procure for oneself. Jesus is saying: "When you pray for something, believe you have *already made it yours*, and you shall have it." We use the word "grasp" to mean taking hold of something mentally as well as physically. Whatever our battle, whether it's for healing, deliverance, finance, or overcoming any obstacle that is standing in the path of our walk with God, we need to grasp what God has delivered. Mark 11:24 tells us clearly that when we have grasped it in the Spirit, we will see it in the flesh.

I think, though, that there is one essential difference between the truth that Jesus was conveying here, and our understanding of the words as framed by our modern, microwave mindset. It may take time for us to lay hold of what has been delivered. It may take more than one prayer, more than one prayer meeting, more than a whole season of prayer meetings. So often we can reach out for God's provision before we have truly received it by faith, then we wonder why we remain empty-handed. Just as we cannot sow seeds onto hard, unprepared ground, we cannot sow seeds of faith on ground that has not been prepared through prayer. It is safe to say that there is no great work of God, in the history of the Church, that has not been preceded by travailing prayer and intercession.

Seeds of faith

Jesus said: "For assuredly, I say to you, if you have faith as a mustard seed, you will say to this mountain, 'Move from here to there,' and it will move; and nothing will be impossible for you" (Matt. 17:20).

The truth is clear. If we can grasp the mustard seed, and if we can plant it, we will receive our delivery. So what is in the seed? First of all, Jesus didn't tell us (Mark 11:22) to have faith IN God; He told us to have the faith OF God. The Greek is the genitive case, denoting possession. To understand "the faith of God", we need to see that it is not a question of dimensions (how could we ever measure anything against God?), but of the type of faith that is being referred to. God spoke the universe into being. God SAID "Let there be . . ." The book of Hebrews tells us that "the worlds were framed by the word of God so that the things which are seen were *not* made of things which are visible" (Heb. 11:3, my emphasis). Jesus spoke "words of life". The faith of God has fully grasped the creative, life-giving power of His word. We know that "faith comes by hearing, and hearing by the (*rhema*) word of God" (Rom. 10:17), but we need to understand the full significance of that statement: when we have received God's word into our lives for a specific situation, the entirety of God's purpose for that situation is contained within it. God tells us through the prophet Isaiah that His word will, without fail, accomplish the purpose for which He sent it. The mustard tree is already in the seed. The faith of God sees the tree, and speaks it forth from the seed.

Cal Pierce writes:

"We must begin to move from having a dependency on the natural world to having a dependency on the spiritual world. After all the spiritual world is more real because it created the natural. This dependency on the spiritual world will cause us to be moved, not by what we see, but what we hear from God. This will change what we see."

(Cal Pierce, *Preparing the Way*, McDougal Publishing, 2003)

The author and finisher of our faith is Jesus. He is the beginning and the end; the Alpha and the Omega. He is the eternal "I am". In Him are past, present and future; creation, Calvary and the New Jerusalem. Our future inheritance is as real in the Spirit as our past salvation, and it is into this inheritance that all the promises of God have been delivered. This is our Hope. When, like Gideon, we look down on our Midianites we hold a seed in our hands in which the victory is delivered, where "no weapon formed against me shall prosper". Whereas we live in the dimension of time, the reality of the Spirit, the dimension of faith, is outside of time. In that dimension, the manifestation of our victory is already unfolding: the Kingdom of God is at hand; the great tree that grows from the mustard seed is right there;

161

the mountain has already been moved into the sea. This is "the substance of things hoped for" (Heb. 11:1). The mustard seed, the faith of God, "gives life to the dead and calls those things which do not exist as though they did" (Rom. 4:17).

I want to look at one more scripture that I find helpful in bringing revelation of this powerful principle. Buried in the treasure trove of Psalm 119 is a verse that the New Living Translation renders thus: "My eyes strain to see your deliverance, to see the truth of your promise fulfilled" (v.123 NLT). We know from 2 Corinthians 1:10 that all God's promises are Yes and Amen in Christ: their fulfilment was sealed at Calvary. That was an historical event. At the same time our inheritance, our hope, is set for a time that, in our dimension, is yet to come: it is the future we travel towards. Meanwhile, in present time, we strain our eyes to see the vision of that inheritance. Past, present and future co-occur. In our hands we hold the mustard seeds that were sown at the cross, and we look into them to see the completed tree. Now imagine a palace. In every room and corridor there is light and power, circuits and appliances, gadgets and gizmos; everything needed for life within its walls. No detail is missing, no need unmet, every eventuality catered for. Running away from the palace is a single power cable, leading to one mains switch. Between that switch and the palace you can see a socket outlet: it will take a single plug. The palace is the Kingdom of God, the New Jerusalem, the future destiny of the Church, "The Promise fulfilled" in completion. The switch is the cross of Calvary. When Jesus threw the switch on the cross, everything in that palace was turned on: there was no time delay. It is blazing now, in all its glory. The socket outlet you can see is yours. When you plug into it, when I plug into mine, the power and provision of that palace is ours in present time.

God wants us to walk in His victory; not to wait for it to happen.

Bible references

Judges 7:9
Proverbs 26:12,16
Isaiah 60:1
1 Corinthians 15:25
Isaiah 53:5
Psalm 34:8
Ephesians 2:8
Mark 11:24
Matthew 17:20
Mark 11:22
Hebrews 11:3
Romans 10:17
Hebrews 11:1
Romans 4:17
Psalm 123:119

Chapter Thirteen
And God Said

Everything that Gideon did as he prepared for battle was preceded by an instruction from the Lord. If we are to lead, we need to hear what God is saying: we need to be listeners.

We cannot short-cut time spent listening to the Holy Spirit, and to listen to Him, we need to be in the Spirit ourselves. This requires an element of discipline, being able to recognise the promptings of the Holy Spirit, and sometimes it means we need to set aside longer periods of "exile" from the daily distractions of our lives to hear His voice more clearly.

n just the first nine verses of Judges 7, the words "The LORD said to Gideon" occur five times. The entire thread of the story up to this point hangs on the ongoing conversation and the growing relationship between Gideon and the Lord, beginning with the presence of God – the Angel of the Lord – breaking into Gideon's world, followed by the instruction to break down the altar to Baal, then the ensuing call to arms and the selection of the 300. We tend to think of the story of Gideon as one of the great examples of God using us in our weakness: Gideon, the weakest member of the weakest clan; the 300, a tiny handful of men against an enemy swarm beyond counting. This is of course a real and important aspect of the narrative, but as we read through the story from the beginning, the recurring theme that stands out most strongly is this: "And God said . . ." Whatever else he may or may not have been, Gideon was a man who listened to the voice of the Lord and did as he was told. He was fearful, he gave expression to his doubts, but all the time he engaged in a dialogue with God and acted on what he heard. When God chose Gideon to be the leader through whom He would bring deliverance, I don't think it was just so that He could demonstrate that "his strength is made perfect in our weakness": I think it was also because He wanted to use Gideon as a demonstration of one of the essential qualities of kingdom leadership: to lead, we have to be listeners.

Verse 11, where God tells Gideon that he would overhear a conversation that would "strengthen his hands" against the Midianites, is the last time in the story where the Lord's words to

167

Gideon are recorded. From this moment on, once Gideon leads his men into battle, we read of his leadership and of the various events that lead to the routing of the Midianite army and the capture of Zebah and Zalmunna, but the Lord is not mentioned again until the very end of the account, when Gideon says that He would rule over them. The record of God's involvement – that aspect which is in the Scriptures for our instruction (Rom. 15:5) – was all in the preparation. The Holy Spirit wants us to see that the victory which has been "delivered" will manifest in our lives when we allow Him fully into the time that leads up to the battle. What is your church – your organisation, your business – facing now? What will you be facing in times to come? How much are we allowing God to speak into those circumstances, and how much time do we spend listening? And probably the biggest question of all: how do we listen?

The unprofitable servant

The Greek word for "obedience" is key here. Paul tell us to take every thought captive "to the obedience of Christ" (2 Cor. 10:5) The word "obedience" used here comes from a root word meaning to "listen attentively" or to "harken" – as, for example, in the duty of a porter, whose duty it is to listen for a knock on the door, then go and open it. It suggests a compliance, an eagerness to respond, so that if we hear a command, we carry it out. In Luke 17:10 Jesus gives us the model of the "unprofitable servant" who exemplifies this attitude: "So likewise you, when you have done all those things which you are commanded, say, 'We are unprofitable servants. We have done what was our duty to do.'"

It is in the context of faith that we are given this illustration. The disciples asked Jesus to increase their faith. He told them that even if they had faith as a grain of mustard seed, they could command the mulberry tree to be uprooted and plant itself on the sea. This is the same "faith of God" that we read of in Mark 11:22-23. We don't need to grow our human capacity to believe what God will do; we need to receive just a grain of the faith that created the universe and release that ourselves. How do we do this? By listening attentively, like the "unprofitable servant", who has no agenda other than to simply do as he is told.

Jesus tells us that His sheep will hear His voice. Isaiah tells us (Isa. 30:21) that we will hear a voice behind us, saying, "This *is* the way, walk in it." We can safely assume that they are both talking about the same voice. So if we believe the word of God, the truth is that the Holy Spirit is talking to us, whether we notice Him or not. Without attempting to offer an exhaustive study of how we can tune our spiritual ears, I believe that the following suggestions may help us to be more attentive to the voice of God.

Traffic lights, peace, and the "voice behind you"

The New Testament contains many references to God's peace. Jesus promises it. His peace "guards our hearts and minds through Christ Jesus" (Phil. 4:7). Exchanging the "sign of peace" with other believers is an important element of Anglican and Catholic liturgy. A real experience of the peace of God given through the Holy Spirit is one assurance of the will of God in a specific circumstance, and young or immature Christians in particular are encouraged to look for God's peace when seeking His will. This does need to be treated with caution, however, as we are all weak and susceptible to deception, particularly in areas where we have a strong idea of what (or maybe "who"!) we want God's answer to be, and the motives of the soul can cast a thick, soft cloak over the truth of God. We read in 2 Corinthians 13:1 that every word shall be established by "two or three witnesses", so the peace that we may feel is best confirmed by another source. At the same time, it is a necessary confirmation if we feel we have heard God speak into a decision through "another witness". On its own it is unreliable, but it is a necessary wavelength to any green light we feel we have been given by the Lord. We must not go without His peace.

Isaiah 30:31 tells us: "Your ears shall hear a word behind you, saying, 'This *is* the way, walk in it,' whenever you turn to the right hand or whenever you turn to the left." Some translations say that we will hear a *voice* behind us. I once heard a minister preaching on this passage from Isaiah 30, who made the point that the voice was behind, not in front. That the "voice" was not so much calling us forward as prompting us from behind, to take a different track from the one that we had just – or were about to – set out on. We are told in Psalm 119:105 that God's word is "a lamp to our feet and a light to our path", and much of what we seek to do as Christians is to walk in the light of God's spiritual laws. We don't need a specific word to tell us which way to go: if we have to make a choice between a course of action that is godly and one that isn't, the decision should not be difficult for us. Other choices, between paths where there isn't one direction where the light of God is clearly shining, may require extended prayer and patience before wisdom is received. And there are also times when the Holy Spirit specifically wants to prompt us to go somewhere or do something that we actually didn't intend to do, but which will bring blessing – and possibly even avoid peril – if we follow His immediate command. This command may just be "Stop!" – a red light, as opposed to a green one, as the next paragraph illustrates.

Thirty-odd years ago a Christian work colleague used to tell the story of the day in 1967 when he was about to get onto a train as a young man and felt strongly that he was being "told" to stay on the platform. The reason he lived to tell the tale is because he obeyed the red light, as the coach he was about to step onto was one of those that was completely destroyed when the train was derailed at Hither Green, near London, killing 47 people in one of the worst rail disasters of the century. Far less dramatic, yet the same "red light", was a small incident that happened just this morning. Anne and I run an educational supplies company. (I used to be a schoolteacher. The colleague I mentioned above was the deputy head of a school I worked at in the 1980s.) I woke early, and saw that Anne was already up. We are in an accounting-deadline period as I write, and it falls to Anne to produce the figures for a quarterly tax return (VAT if you are in Europe). She is under pressure, because there are heavy fines for non-compliance and her life is full enough without VAT, and she often sleeps badly while she is working on them. I knew that she was downstairs at her computer. I lay in bed for a few minutes, trying to decide whether I might just manage to go back to sleep, or whether to get up and spend an extra hour on this book. As the inexorable tide of wakefulness gradually broke over my consciousness I decided, reluctantly, to give up on the sleep option, and threw back the covers to get out of bed. Immediately I felt a red light. "Not yet." "Lord, you are so good to me!" I thought and settled back down under the covers. Less than a minute later, I heard footsteps on the stairs and Anne came back to bed. She had been working half the night, had an appointment later this morning, but was going to get a bit more rest now. She told me what time she needed to be up, I got out of bed, and she shut her eyes.

Of course we could have had that conversation on the stairs (as one waited for the other to pass) or while she was at her desk (interrupting her train of thought), but this way was perfect: a smooth transition, a simple switching of points. I didn't get my lie-in, but actually this was much more satisfying, because I felt that I had heard the Lord and responded to Him, and thus was in His perfect will – at least for this period of time. And although it seems unlikely, who knows what interruption could have occurred, what careless word may have been spoken and what damage done if I had not taken notice of that red light and gone down my intended track? We never know what train crash God is sparing us from when He changes our direction.

Sometimes God will give us a nudge just because He loves us and wants to spare us discomfort – although if we reflect on these promptings we can often find a deeper significance if we choose to look. We get a lot of birds in our garden, and I put feeders out for them, filled with sunflower seeds. I normally top up the feeders in the morning. It's a slightly fiddly operation, involving the removal of an anti-squirrel (or in our case, anti-crow) cage before accessing the seed hopper. The other evening, while I was out in the garden, the thought dropped into my head to "do the bird feeders now". "Good idea," I thought, and did just that, then carried on with what I was doing. The following morning it was pouring with rain. If I had left the feeders until then, either I would have got soaked, or the birds would have missed their breakfast.

In His love for me, and for the birds of His creation, God didn't want either of those to happen. But as I said, we can often find a prophetic significance in the details of events like this as well. This said to me that God wants to keep us topped up with seeds from His storehouse, so that we are always ready to sow the word of God into other people's lives. If our hoppers are empty when the rainstorms come we will have nothing to draw on, for ourselves, or for others.

Warriors in training

The point is this: we are warriors in training. The only way we can learn to clearly hear the instructions of our Commander is to learn to listen for His voice. We can do this through practice. Jesus teaches us in the parable of the talents that if we are faithful in "small things" we will be given greater responsibilities. We can apply this to our faithfulness in responding to these simple "voices behind us" – the red light and green light commands. The truth is that God is speaking to us – at times directly by his Spirit, at other times through angels ("ministering spirits sent to serve those who will inherit salvation" Heb. 1:14 NIV) – our task is to learn to discern which of the voices in our heads belongs to Him. Try it. Here are two scenarios. You are about to drive off to work. You think, "I'm sure I've forgotten something." Scenario one: you go through your checklist. Wallet – phone – lunch (that's mine). You think – No, got it all – put it out of your mind, and head for work. As a result you miss the phone call from the old friend who rang two minutes after you left to see if you had time for a coffee later in the day, as he was going to be passing by. The voice in your head wasn't anything to do with what you might have forgotten; that was just your interpretation of a basic red light. God was saying stop. He doesn't usually say why. Scenario two: you recognise the red light, and instead of trying to interpret it with your own thoughts, you say: "Lord, was there something else?", and you stop and go back into the house. Result – you get the phone call and meet your old friend. While you have that coffee it turns out that he needs to unburden his heart on a personal matter, and the result is that you lead him to the Lord – after praying for him for the last fifteen years. When God is changing the points, we simply do not know what is down the track.

Of course there will be many times when we conjure up "promptings" from our own imaginations. We can tell when this is the case, because nothing comes of them; whereas when it is from the Lord, He usually lets us see the result. Why? Because He wants us to learn, and there is nothing more encouraging than "getting it right". To learn the lessons we have to make mistakes, but gradually we do learn to discern the voice of our Shepherd. The "voice behind us" is one of the restoration promises to Israel that is ours to receive as Jesus builds His Kingdom today. In the same chapter of Isaiah, we are told that our teachers "would not be in a corner any more" (v.20), but would be visible to our eyes. If we commit ourselves to God's classroom in simple everyday actions, we will "see" Him at work, instructing us, preparing us for those "greater things" as He leads us into battle.

In the Spirit on the Lord's Day

There is so much more to the topic of hearing God than can be covered in the few pages of this chapter. Most important is that we spend time "in the Spirit". John was "in the Spirit on the Lord's Day" – when he heard the voice of Jesus Christ behind him – "a loud voice, as of a trumpet" (Rev. 1:10) – and what followed was the book of Revelation. He heard the voice before he saw the vision. (Interestingly enough, the voice was behind him, in keeping with Isaiah 30:21). We do not know exactly what John meant by saying he was "in the Spirit", but what is unlikely is the very thing that is often assumed from a casual reading of the scripture: i.e. that he was already in some state of trance before he received the revelation. Some (non-Christian) commentators even suggest that this trance was induced by hallucinogenic drugs. But any reading of the New Testament will show us that the phrase "in the Spirit" is not used to refer to extraordinary spiritual experiences, but to the everyday realities of Christian life. Over 20 verses in the NT refer to living, walking, groaning, praying and speaking mysteries "in the Spirit". Jesus gives John a very specific instruction: "Write the things which you have seen, and the things which are, and the things which will take place after this" (Rev. 1:19). Although John writes elsewhere (Rev. 4:2; 17:3; 21:10) of being transported "in the Spirit" to other dimensions, the details recorded in the book that he was told to write begin with the vision of Jesus that John saw after he had heard the loud voice behind him, suggesting that the words "in the Spirit" refer to his condition before the vision began. If that is the case, it implies that whatever John was doing then is also accessible to the rest of us.

We have already covered the usefulness of praying in tongues if we want our spiritual ears to be tuned into divine frequencies. Mahesh Chavda, a man who has led multiple thousands of people to Jesus, through whom the dead have been raised and the Lord has brought about many miraculous healings, has written an entire book on this gift: *The Hidden Power of Speaking in Tongues*. There are many other books on the subject, a seminal work from the charismatic era probably being *They Speak with Other Tongues* by John and Elizabeth Sherill, published in the late 1970s. Maybe John was praying in tongues at the time.

Fasting is strongly associated with spiritual sensitivity: in the Old Testament, the revelations of Daniel are preceded by his protracted "vegetable fast" (what Ben Goldacre, in his book *Bad*

Science, calls the first controlled trial in human history). Jesus preceded His ministry with forty days of fasting. The entire ministry of John the Baptist was characterised by a lifestyle of fasting. Paul and Barnabas were commissioned when the Holy Spirit spoke to the church during a time of worship and fasting (Acts 13:2-3). Jesus is clear (e.g. Matt. 17:21) that fasting is part of the fabric of a powerful prayer life. Mahesh Chavda (again) regularly carries out forty-day fasts, but for those of us who have not progressed nearly as far along that path of spiritual discipline, even a few hours – one skipped meal – can make a difference. I recall two occasions this year, when our church was running a café in the local park, where I felt the Holy Spirit told me not to eat breakfast, and then to go down to the café – not to eat, but just to be there. On both occasions I sensed specific leadings, first to go and sit at a particular table, and second not to leave the café when I was about to, which resulted in meaningful conversations which could (and hopefully will) have significant Kingdom implications within the local community. This sort of leading is commonplace in the Spirit-led life: I only draw attention to them here because these little mini-fasts are probably the level that most of us are more likely to operate on. The point is that God will use them to tune our ears to His voice. Maybe John was fasting as well.

How else could John have been "in the Spirit"? Unlike the Church in the book of Acts, who were "fasting and ministering to the Lord" (i.e. worshipping) when Saul and Barnabas were commissioned by the Holy Spirit , we know that John could not have been engaged in any corporate worship because he was exiled alone on the Isle of Patmos. However, he may have been – and probably was – worshipping God in his personal devotions at the time. What we know is true is that he had no distractions, other than seeing to his basic life needs, so he had extra time to spend with the Lord. John "was on the island that is called Patmos for the word of God and for the testimony of Jesus Christ" (Rev. 1:9), and Jesus, who had planned it anyway, met with him there. He needed John to be exiled for him to be given the end of the Bible. We too need to make sure that we have times on our own "Island of Patmos", exiled away from distractions, so that we can meet with the Lord.

For us, every day is the Lord's day. The example of John is there for all of us: if we want revelation; if we want, like Gideon, to receive clear and specific instructions from the God of angel armies, we need to spend time in the Spirit.

Bible references

Romans 15:5
Judges 7:11
2 Corinthians 10:5
Luke 17:10
Isaiah 30:21
Philippians 4:7
2 Corinthians 13:1
Psalm 119:105
Hebrews 1:14
Isaiah 30:20

Revelation 1:10
Revelation 1:19
Revelation 4:2; 17:3; 21:10
Acts 13:2-3
Matthew 17:21
Revelation 1:9

Chapter Fourteen
God's Symphony

God knows the frailties of our hearts and the limits of our faith, but He also wants us to be real about them with Him. He orchestrated events so that Gideon's faith would be strengthened by overhearing a conversation between two of the Midianites about a dream one of them had during the night.

Sometimes a fresh revelation of God's mind-bending reach and sovereign control beyond the tiny dimensions of human existence is what we need to increase our faith and courage.

love how God orchestrates our lives. Most of the time we are not aware of it, but sometimes He lets us hear a few chords. As I was writing about concrete earlier, builders were working at the house next door, and I heard the distinct sound of concrete being scraped off the ground with a shovel. I haven't heard it since, and I hadn't heard it before then; but just as I was writing that particular section, it was as though God was providing a soundtrack to reinforce the significance of that event. Of course there are many people who would say that was a coincidence. Personally, I would call it God's symphony. There are many accounts in the Bible narrative where we see the Master Conductor at work, such as in the story of Esther, where one chord after another is played as unconnected events come together to bring about the destruction of the enemy's plans and the fulfilment of God's purposes. As Gideon moves on from his vantage point above the enemy camp, he too is shown just how God is orchestrating events.

What does God say to Gideon at this point? "But if you are afraid to go down, go down to the camp with Purah your servant, and you shall hear what they say; and afterward your hands shall be strengthened to go down against the camp" (Judg. 7:10-11). If you are afraid. This is the second time in the narrative that God has recognised the reality of fear. He had already sent home 22,000 warriors who were trembling in their boots. God knows our human frame: He made it. Although we are exhorted throughout the Bible to "Fear not", there are also times when God does not expect us to just "get a grip" of our fears. Each of us has been given a measure of faith (Rom. 12:3), and while we are genuinely living out of the measure of faith that we have been dealt there is no room for fear – "For God has not given us a spirit of fear, but *of power* and of *love* and of a *sound mind*" (2 Tim. 1:7). However, there are times when the circumstances that we face require a provision of God's grace that takes us beyond that measure. At this point, we need to be real with God, who sees our hearts anyway, and tell Him our fears and our uncertainties. This is where we cry out with the father of the deaf and dumb boy (Mark 9:24), "Lord, I believe; help my unbelief!"

Fresh revelation

What we need, what Gideon needed, is fresh revelation. Up to this point, Gideon had not actually engaged with the enemy; he had only believed in the possibility of victory, even victory through his little band of 300, but he had not yet faced an enemy blade. Now it was the reality of his next step. This was no longer the church leadership presenting the vision of the next mission; this was stepping out to preach the gospel on the streets. This was reality, and this is where we need to be real with God, and with each other. If we need more faith, now is the time to say so. Our faith cannot depend on another person's revelation, and it cannot depend on our mental assent to the teachings we have received: faith comes from hearing, and hearing from the word of God that is sown into our hearts. For, as Paul tells us in Romans 10:10, it is with the heart that we believe; we do not believe with our heads. The father of the boy with the deaf and dumb spirit knew in his head ("I believe") that Jesus could cast out the demon, because the testimonies had gone before Him; but he recognised that there was unbelief in his heart ("help my unbelief"). There are all too many shipwrecks of faith that ran aground on the rocks of belief that did not reside in the heart.

God knew Gideon's heart, and He gave him the opportunity to face and overcome the fear that still dwelt there. He invited Gideon to step into His orchestra. We cannot increase our own measure of faith, however much we pray or study the word. Faith is a gift from God, and it is God who determines the measure that we receive. However, since, like Paul, "We have not already attained, but press on toward the goal of the upward call of God in Christ Jesus" (Phil. 3:14), God will increase that measure as we move nearer the goal. "Come with me," He says, "and I will pull aside a corner of the curtain so you can get a glimpse of just how much I am actually in control of my universe."

So, acting on a new word from God, Gideon moves even closer to the blade of the enemy; close enough to eavesdrop on the conversation between two guards, and it is only now that he finally "gets it". As Gideon approaches, what he sees is the enemy massed along the valley like grains of sand on the seashore. If they seemed many beforehand, the reality from where he now stood was even more intimidating. But what he hears, because God had so orchestrated the circumstances, was a conversation in which an enemy guard is telling his companion of a dream in which a loaf of barley bread crushed a Midianite tent, which his companion says is nothing other than the sword of Gideon destroying the Midianites (Judg. 7:14). Because Gideon has been real with God about his fears and still taken another step forward within the measure of faith that he has been given, God has shown Gideon a higher reality in which he, Gideon, is the destroyer, and it is the enemy who is overturned.

The illusion room

There are optical illusion rooms created by tricking the eye with patterns of stripes, where a small child can stand next to a grown man and appear taller than him. Our human perceptions are limited to the dimensions of space and time. God, who created these dimensions as the framework for our existence, lives outside them; and in the Bible we do get glimpses of a reality where the fabric of our four-dimensional world of space and time is burst open like a paper bag. In Acts 8:26-40, for example, Philip is instantly transported from one place to another after explaining to the Ethiopian Eunuch the meaning of the passage he was reading in the book of Isaiah: space and time were simply folded around God's purpose. Paul was taken to the seventh Heaven: what dimension could that be in? Our dimensions are like the stripes in that illusion room. They serve their purpose in our earthly life, but the Christian is a new creation, born again of the Spirit of God; when we face our enemy, when we face that obstacle, however big it may appear, the truth is the reality without the stripes: the obstacle is the size of the child, and you and I are the adult in authority. God folded the universe for Gideon and removed the stripes, and Gideon finally had the revelation of who he really was: "This *is* nothing else but the sword of Gideon the son of Joash, a man of Israel! Into his hand God has delivered Midian and the whole camp" (Judg. 7:14).

God's orchestration of His purposes applies across every detail of our lives. If we are committed to Him and the extension of His Kingdom, the most trivial moments of our day can be relevant to the unfolding of a greater work that He is preparing in unseen realms. There is no such thing as coincidence. This is why God really can, and does, "give us parking places". Such an "unspiritual" and self-seeking prayer as a request for a spot in a busy car park is a regular object of mockery in non-Christian and even some church circles, but how many of us have regularly seen this prayer answered? I certainly have. In the multiplicity of interlocking events that create cause and effect on our planet, who can count how many times a timely parking spot leads to a quicker shopping trip that means a phone call is answered that leads to a conversation that leads . . . who knows where? Or conversely the fact that I have this parking place means that person x has to spend longer waiting, which sets off a different chain of events for that individual. One person, and one only, does indeed know, and He is the Creator of all things. If it is in His timing, whether or not we are aware of it, for us to park the car quickly and conveniently, He will orchestrate events so that we do. God chose to give Philip a short cut through time and space when he had preached the gospel to the Ethiopian eunuch, but at other times He will achieve equally significant results through the combination of a series of exactly-planned steps executed by a number of individuals working unknowingly together.

Anne had to go into hospital this week for an invasive operation on her digestive tract. Needless to say, her emotions were a mixture of anxiety and trust in the Lord. What is the verse she comes to in her daily reading on the morning of her surgery? None other than Jer. 29:11 (NIV): "'For I know the plans I have for you,' declares the LORD, 'plans to prosper you and not to harm you, plans to give you hope and a future.'" Most of us who walk with the Lord have had these "How does He do that?" times, when the scripture we find ourselves coming to in the sequence of our daily reading lines up exactly with a specific situation we are facing, bringing us encouragement and reassurance of His presence with us.

The orchestra

Unbelief calls such alignments of differing strands of circumstance mere coincidence, since any other explanation calls into question a purely naturalist worldview. Some non-Christian thinkers have tried to embrace the existence of the inexplicable, and even explain it within the context of their own philosophical or pseudo-scientific models: Karl Jung created the idea of the "Collective Unconscious" and Arthur Koestler wrote about "The Ghost in the Machine", to name but two: I am sure there are many others whose work I haven't read or even heard of. But Hebrews 1:3 tells us that Jesus, the Son of God, "[upholds] all things by the word of His power". When the word of God is delivered into our lives with such relevance and clarity by the Holy Spirit and by no other human agency; when two apparently independent strands of existence suddenly become so fused into one that scripture is suddenly and supernaturally stamped over our circumstance – I believe that these are moments when time and space and anything we can measure are completely by-passed, and we are connecting directly into the power that "upholds all things" – every dimension, every strand of circumstance, every atom in the universe. In his book *A brief History of Time* scientist Stephen Hawking attempts to unravel what the film about his life calls "The Theory of Everything". But without an acceptance of the true power that upholds all things – the same power that not only orchestrates but speaks directly and personally into the daily lives of His friends (for such He calls us!) – even the most complex models of the greatest scientists in the world are the one-dimensional scribbles of a small child; Lego-brick constructions on the playroom floor.

The wings of the morning

I would like to record one more chord in God's orchestra. Someone I know has a close relative who is a fast jet pilot with the US marines. On the morning that the pilot was due to fly from the air base to the aircraft carrier for his first operational tour, my friend opened the Bible for his daily reading. The psalm he read for that day was psalm 139, David's beautiful words that tell how we cannot escape from God's love, how wonderfully he has made us, how He knows all things about us. Verses 9-10 say this: "*If* I take the wings of the morning, *and* dwell in the uttermost parts of the sea, even there Your hand shall lead me, and Your right hand shall hold me." He was able to give this promise to the pilot before he left. Could anything in the whole of the Bible be more specific, and more encouraging, for a young man who loves the Lord and is about to fly out in the morning to spend the next few months of his life living on an aircraft carrier "in the uttermost parts of the sea"? These words could have been written for him, and there they were, ready to be delivered at the exact time of his need, by somebody who had "just happened" to reach that chapter in his daily readings. How God arranges such synchronicity is indeed beyond any understanding that we can frame with human dimensions. The psalmist himself is attempting to express the wonder of God's omniscience and omnipresence just two verses earlier in the same psalm, when he writes: "You have hedged me behind and before, and laid Your hand upon me. *Such* knowledge *is* too wonderful for me; it is high, I cannot *attain* it" (Ps. 139:5-6).

Whatever our circumstances, whether we are fighting the Midianites, flying an aeroplane or parking a car, God has moved events around so that we can be part of His Kingdom purposes and become who He has called us to be. We really are "fearfully and wonderfully made", and the Spirit of God is at work in and through all things. "In Him we live and move and have our being" (Acts 17:28). We must check, as warriors, that our understanding of circumstances and events is not tainted by the limitations of naturalist thinking. As we listen attentively for His word and open our eyes to His supernatural work, God will increase our measure of the real, mustard seed "faith of God" that Gideon finally received, and which changes the course of human events.

Bible references

Judges 7:10-11

Romans 12:3

2 Timothy 1:7

Mark 9:24

Romans 10:10

Philippians 3:14

Judges 7:14

Acts 8:26-40

Jeremiah 29:11

Hebrews 1:3

Psalm 139:9-10

Psalm 139:5-6

Acts 17:28

Chapter Fifteen
He Worshipped

When Gideon had the revelation that God had truly given him the victory, he fell down and worshipped. David learned a hard lesson when he brought the Ark into Jerusalem: flesh and blood do not bring the presence of God into our midst. Worship comes out of a revelation of Jesus. If we want the Ark among us, we must have a real understanding of what it means to worship in the beauty of holiness; in spirit and in truth.

"They shall be like mighty men, who tread down their enemies in the mire of the streets in the battle. They shall fight because the Lord is with them, and the riders on horses shall be put to shame." (Zech.10:5)

The prophet Zechariah writes these words about Judah. When Leah gave birth to Judah, she said, "Now I will praise the Lord" (Gen. 29:35). Judah means praise. As brothers and sisters, by adoption, of the Lion of the Tribe of Judah, the promise for all of us who praise the Lord is that we will be like mighty men, and fight because the Lord is with us. As we have seen, the first part of the story of Gideon leads us to the place where he finally realises that he actually is the "mighty man of valour" that was first addressed by the angel in Judges 6:12. Gideon is exactly who God says he is, just as we are who God says we are. What was Gideon's response?

> "And so it was, when Gideon heard the telling of the dream and its interpretation, that he worshipped."
>
> (Judg. 7:15)

He worshipped. As everywhere else in scripture, the timing is meaningful. This is the first point in the story where we see Gideon worshipping God, so we need to ask ourselves why. It is also the pivotal moment, the tipping point, because in the following verse we read of how he equips the 300 for the attack. If we flip to the New Testament and Matthew 28:17, we see another revelation on another mountain, when the risen Jesus came to the gathered disciples before the Great Commission and His ascension: "When they saw Him, they worshipped Him, but some doubted." The command to "Go into all the world" was preceded by a revelation of the risen Lord, and worship. We "go" from the place of worship. The alternative is doubt. We don't hear of the exploits of all the eleven who were present here – maybe they were the ones that doubted?

Worship is central to victory over our Midianites, and central to our mission to take the gospel to the nations. The word used here, the most frequent term for worship in the OT, is *Shachah*, which means to bow down or prostrate oneself. The commonest word for praise is *Tehillah*, which expresses adoration and thanksgiving, and is a response to the qualities, deeds or attributes of God. Throughout the Bible, and the OT in particular, the two threads of praise and worship are closely intertwined, as indeed are the themes of praise and battle: Psalm 149 puts a sword in our hands and praise in our mouths, and in 2 Chronicles 20:20 the worship team marched ahead of the army and saw the Lord give victory to Jehoshaphat over the Moabites and the Ammonites. At the time of Jehoshaphat's battle the Levites were instructed to "praise Him for the splendour of His holiness", and in Psalm 29:2 we are exhorted to "Give unto the Lord the glory due to His name; worship the Lord in the beauty of holiness". Praise, worship, and victory: at the core is the beauty of God's holiness.

Although praise and worship are different expressions of our response to the Lord's attributes and His love for us, and in particular to "the Beauty of His holiness", we need to understand the relationship between the two if we are to be in the same place as Gideon as we go into battle. This is particularly true in our church services, where an incomplete understanding of the two terms can mean that they are both used more or less interchangeably and can lead to a lack of intimacy with God and ensuing Holy Spirit power.

Praise, *Shachah*, is the only fitting response that can be made to the deeds, the attributes or the qualities of God. His splendour and glory are aptly summed up in the phrase that we have already quoted: "the beauty of His holiness". As Jesus said on His approach to Jerusalem: the stones themselves would cry out (Luke 19:40) if the crowds who were shouting His praise were to keep silent. Praise can be sung, or shouted, or expressed in a number of other ways such as clapping, playing musical instruments, or dancing – references to all of these can be found in scripture. What they all have in common is that they are energetic and wholehearted responses to an awareness of God's glory. Praise is not muted or reserved. If even the stones would cry out, the trees "clap their hands" (Isa. 55:12) or the "mountains sing . . . for Joy" (Ps. 98:8 NIV) at the coming of the Lord, then the response of our redeemed new hearts must surely be even more enraptured.

Another aspect of praise is that it is usually public or corporate, whereas worship is about our personal response to God. Worship may be expressed in public, but public worship exists only insofar as individual hearts are joined in their personal response to Jesus. Praise, on the other hand, in which God is exalted, can be and usually is corporate. It can often precede worship, as it can bring an awareness of the Divine Nature to our hearts when they were previously far from Him, and bring about the sense of prostration before His throne that is at the heart of worship. But whether or not praise brings us to our knees it must, as King David discovered, carry with it a true understanding and reverence for the mighty power of the presence of God. Gideon's journey to worship was launched at the outset by the manifest presence of God – the appearance of the Angel of the Lord. Most of us have to take a different route, but it is still the presence of God that we need to seek.

David's journey

By the end of 2 Samuel 5 we have read – through the lens of David's rise to power – the story of a successful church. The church (the City of David) is built and relationships are strong (David "built inward" – v.9). The church family is growing (v.13-16). The leader is esteemed in the wider community (v.11). Battles are being won (vs.17-25). Verse 10 sums up this stage in David's life: "David went on and became great, and the LORD God of hosts was with him." Nevertheless, something was missing: even though David and the people of Israel were established in Jerusalem, the Ark was up on a hill at the house of Abinadab. The name "Abinadab" means "My father is noble" or "My father is willing": we can acknowledge God's greatness, we can pray "Thy will be done", and our church can be strong and successful; but

God can still be remote; His presence far away on a distant hill. King David knew that the presence of God had to be at the heart of his city, so he "arose and went with all the people who *were* with him from Baale Judah to bring up from there the ark of God, whose name is called by the Name, the Lord of Hosts, who dwells *between* the cherubim" (2 Sam. 6:2). David's heart was after God, and this was the right decision to make. He had the right idea – but he had some important lessons to learn in its execution; lessons which are there for the edification of all of us. We all know what happened a little bit down the road – one of the oxen slipped, Uzzah put his hand out to steady the ark, and God struck him dead. But it's easy to miss the place where it began to unravel, because it wasn't so much Uzzah's action that caused his death, as the attitudes and assumptions that led up to it.

So where did it all go wrong? Verse 3 gives us the clue:

> "So they set the ark of God on a new cart, and brought it out of the house of Abinadab, which *was* on the hill; and Uzzah and Ahio, the sons of Abinadab, drove the new cart."

Now fast forward 3,000-odd years, and let's listen in on the elders of a successful city church somewhere in the 21st century . . . "We need to do something about the worship. It's good, but people aren't getting into the Spirit. God isn't showing up like He used to/like He does down the road/like in the Book of Acts (take your pick or make up your own). We need to bring some freshness into the worship group; maybe make a few changes, bring in some of the younger generation." Or: "We need to put the Ark on a new cart, and let the sons of Abinadab lead it."

The presence of God cannot be ushered in by the skill of the musicians or the charisma and energy of the worship leader: it is only through sensitivity to the Holy Spirit's leading and willingness to give time to His agenda that worship leaders can bring a congregation into "The Holy Place". God wants to know what our priorities are, and if we place our timetable above His we cannot be surprised if He doesn't "show up" in our meetings. One of the most powerful times of praise and worship that I have been part of recently consisted of one hour and twenty minutes of varied expressions of praise and worship including singing in English and in tongues, marching round the room, the use of banners, and prophetic declarations. This was followed by a period of total silence which lasted seven or eight minutes, during which time many people were prostrate in adoration. It could be said that the Ark was in the room at this time. The silence was eventually broken by a long and weighty prophecy which related God's intentions for the members of the group in a global context. This took place at a conference. The teaching that was planned for that session was never given: instead, we met with God.

The weight of the Ark

So the "New Cart" means nothing to the Holy Spirit, and will make no difference to the anointing on our praise and worship. In fact God's instructions to Moses regarding transportation of the Ark made no reference to any kind of cart, but to poles on the shoulders of the priests. We read in 1 Chronicles that the Levites had to carry the Ark of God with poles on their shoulders, according to the commandment that Moses had received from the Lord. The Levitical ministry required a lifetime of holiness and purity: failure and compromise was punishable by death. Under the new covenant Jesus has taken the penalty for our sin upon Himself, but we worship the same holy God as the sons of Aaron. Just as the shoulders of the priests carried the physical weight of the Ark (dense wood; solid gold – hardly an aluminium-framed rucksack) in OT times, there is a spiritual weight today to our ministry as a holy priesthood. It is when we count the cost and pick up the weight of a consecrated lifestyle and a commitment to prayer that we will see the presence of God carried into our meetings. We cannot expect the Ark to roll in just because the wheels of our cart – new or old – are turning.

David reveals that he has learnt his lesson in 1 Chronicles 15:13 (NIV): "It was because you, the Levites, did not bring it up the first time that the Lord our God broke out in anger against us. We did not inquire of Him how to do it in the prescribed way."

Abinadab and his sons were descendants of Levi, and therefore were rightful keepers of the Ark under the Law of Moses. However, Uzzah and Ahio were clearly not consecrated for the task, operating instead in pride ("we're the ones who are leading the cart") and presumption ("the honour falls to us, as the Ark has been in our father's house"). In the grace of God there are no prescribed laws that need to be fulfilled to come into His presence, yet the lesson of consecration remains: God is the same yesterday, today and tomorrow.

Equally telling are two other details that relate to this incident. The story of the rise of David and the fall of Saul is a picture of another battle that we read about in the NT – the war between the Spirit and the flesh. The story of David is the story of the spiritual battle faced by every Christian who is seeking to become more like Jesus. Worship is a spiritual activity: God seeks worshippers who will worship "in spirit and in truth". However, Abinadab was a son of fleshly Saul. The flesh cannot usher in the presence of God. When the Ark seems to be falling off the cart and the service does not seem to be going in the direction desired, when the congregation aren't "getting into worship", fleshly attempts to whip up enthusiasm will only lead to death. And the new cart: that was actually based on the Philistine way of transporting their sacred objects. If the flesh is leading us astray, the world is usually not far behind, and over them both, of course, is the devil. The greatest talent and best technology and systems in the world will not bring us into the throne-room of God. How the devil loves it when we rely on them.

David learned – and teaches us – some hard lessons on the journey from Kiriath Jeharim, but when the Ark eventually reached Jerusalem the tabernacle was set up, and for forty years a New Testament principle was enacted: the "sacrifice of praise". Jesus told the woman at the well that "we worship what we know" (John 4:22). Gideon had received revelation of who God was and what God had done for him. As we come into the tabernacle and praise our God, declaring His glory and His attributes, we remind ourselves of who He is and of what Jesus has done for each one of us at the cross, but this corporate act at the tabernacle of the Presence is still not worship and does not of itself transport us to the place of victory where Gideon found himself. Worship arises in the body of Christ when we as individuals have prostrated ourselves before the God who made the universe and who has lifted us into His presence through the cross.

Psalm 149:6 teaches us that the enemy is defeated when we have the "high praises of God . . . in our mouths and a two edged sword in [our] hands". The Father seeks those who will worship in spirit and truth. It seems that these two statements, one from the OT and one from the NT, are in sync with each other: when we praise God in the revealed truth of His greatness, our spirits are lifted in worship, and it is at this place that the Ark of God comes into the room, borne on the shoulders of the New Testament priesthood; that the chains fall off the prisoners, and, just as Gideon did, we move into the victory that Jesus has won for us. Like the disciples at the Ascension, if we want to hear what God is commanding us today, let us go to the mountain and worship.

Bible references

Zechariah 10:5

Genesis 29:35

Judges 7:15

Matthew 28:17

Psalm 149

2 Chronicles 20:20

Psalm 29:2

Luke 19:40

Isaiah 55:12

Psalm 98:8

2 Samuel 5

2 Samuel 6:2

1 Chronicles 15:13

John 4:22

Psalm 149:6

Chapter Sixteen
Declaring the Victory

Having worshipped God in the revelation of the victory that was given to him, Gideon declared it to his men in faith. Faith calls us to know the reality of God's provision before we walk into it. However, the declaration of our "seeds of faith" requires that we submit to the cross: the death of self is the only fertile ground for the seeds of the Kingdom of God.

It was at the place of worship that Gideon declared the victory. Judges 7:15 (niv) tells us that after he had worshipped, "He returned to the camp of Israel and called out: 'Get up! The Lord has given the Midianite camp into your hands.'" No-one leading an army will want to go into battle from a position of weakness: forces are equipped with weapons for defence and attack; enemy positions are bombarded by airstrikes and artillery before the forces on the ground move in. Our position of greatest strength is when, in worship, we know the presence of the God who is our strength and our song (as in Ps. 118 and Isa. 12, for example). Gideon's declaration of faith at this point was more than encouragement to the troops: they were words of power that had an impact in the spirit realm. When Paul writes of the weapons of our spiritual warfare that are mighty through God to pull down strongholds (2 Cor. 10:4) we must be careful not to limit our thinking to "warfare prayer" and the casting out of demons: prophetic declarations of faith springing forth from our worship are powerful weapons against the enemy, and in the advancement of the purposes of our King. The times when we are lifted high in our worship can sometimes be the very moments to drop bombs on our enemy. These bombs are our declarations of the victory that we have already received.

As we saw in chapter twelve, we are to both believe for, and receive, God's provision. But we are also to declare it. In Psalm 2:7 the psalmist writes prophetically:

"I will declare the decree: The Lord has said to Me, 'You are My Son, today I have begotten You.'"

This verse looks forward to Jesus the Messiah, but it also speaks to us. Everything the Lord says to us can be called a decree, for we know that His word is settled in Heaven, and that it does not return to Him void, but will accomplish the purpose for which He sent it. Job 22:28 tells us: "You will also declare a thing, and it will be established for you; so light will shine on your ways." If we believe, as scripture tells us, that the word of God is the power that holds the universe together, we must surely believe that declaring it over our situations will release something of that power into our lives.

However, I don't believe that the Bible teaches us a "promise-box theology", whereby the utterance of the verses alone have some talismanic effect. It is easy to look up a promise that speaks into our situation, claim it for ourselves, expect circumstances to line up accordingly, then be disappointed when they don't. Hebrews 4:2 teaches us that it isn't the word alone that achieves God's purpose, but it is the word "mixed with faith" that "profits" us. When God sends a word that will not return to Him void, it is a specific word for a specific purpose. These unstoppable seeds of creative purpose range from the great promises of restoration that are incorporated in the canon of scripture, to personal words of encouragement or direction that are delivered and confirmed to individuals in a local church context. Faith is the good ground on which these seeds are sown. God is a god of relationship. Although everything in His word is true for all of us all the time, it is activated in our lives when the Holy Spirit breathes His life into it for a specific purpose, and when we co-operate by living in obedience to His will.

Live seeds

Job was a man whose declarations would be established, but Job was also the most outstanding example (other than the Lord Jesus) of integrity in the whole of scripture. A person who walks in integrity is one whose life lines up with his words. We can hardly expect to speak the words of God and see them fulfilled if our lives are not going to line up behind them. This does not diminish in any way the grace of God, or suggest that the fulfilment of God's promises depends on anything other than the complete work of the cross, but underlines the fact that the kingdom to which we are called is one of light, freedom, good fruit and good works; and our loving Father is waiting to give His kingdom to all who will allow His grace to work in their lives. And although that love is unconditional, and that grace is complete, Jesus is clear about the one condition He does require if our promise box is to contain live seeds and not empty husks: He calls us to pick up our cross daily and follow Him. We cannot receive His life unless we die to our own. The seed cannot become the tree it contains unless it falls to the ground and embraces death. All "these things" will only be given to us (Matt. 6:33) if we seek the Kingdom of God above our own desires. If we want to be connected to the power of God's decrees, we have to be connected to the cross.

All of this leads to an inescapable fact: declaring the word of God "in faith" requires more than selecting a promise to fit our circumstances and expecting it to come true because we've said so. As we will see in the next chapter, Gideon's victory was first manifest when the light was revealed, and the light was only revealed when the jars were broken. The apostle Peter was a man who most definitely "walked the walk", and he tells us clearly in his second letter that faith was something to be "added to" by other qualities – specifically virtue, knowledge, self-control, perseverance, godliness, brotherly kindness and love. He tells us that if we don't possess all of these that we are blind and forgetting that we have been cleansed of our sins; but that if we are diligent to possess them *all* we will "never stumble", and an "entrance will be supplied to you abundantly into the ever-lasting kingdom of our Lord and Saviour Jesus Christ" (2 Pet. 1:5-11).

So what is to "supply an entrance abundantly into the Kingdom of God"? We know that Christ's completed work on the cross has paid the full price of our citizenship of the Kingdom of God; that it is His blood and not our renewed minds and godly characters that have purchased our eternal life and given us that place in Heaven where all the promises of God will be fulfilled. Our salvation is not dependent on whether or not we stumble. I believe the entrance that Peter is writing about here is the same as the one that Jesus is describing when He tells us that He is the door, or the gate, to the sheepfold; and that through Him we go "in and out and find pasture" once we have found salvation in Him (John 10:9). I believe that Peter – who would have heard these very words from Christ's lips – is writing about a door that is held wide open for us ("an entrance supplied abundantly") to pass through every time we need to bring divine resources into the human realm: when we want to bring Heaven to earth; in other words when we want to see God's will (for salvation, healing, restoration, deliverance, provision, etc.) done on earth as it is in Heaven.

The keys to the Kingdom

Jesus gave Peter the keys to the Kingdom (Matt. 16:19). Through these keys, whatever is bound, or loosed, on Earth will have been bound or loosed in heaven. I believe that the attributes that Peter writes about in verses 5-11 are these very keys: they unlock the door and hold it wide open for us; the abundant supply of repeated entrance into the realms of Heaven, to build the Kingdom of God on this Earth. They are not a mystical bunch on a golden chain that St Peter jangles as he sits on his chair by the pearly gates: they are faith, virtue, knowledge, self-control, perseverance, godliness, brotherly kindness and love. They are ours to lay hold of, given to us out of His grace in the measure that we partake of His divine nature through the "great and precious promises" that are ours.

It is "through faith and patience" that we inherit these promises (Heb. 6:12), all of which we know are yes and amen in Christ. It takes patience to add these keys to the faith that tells us God's promises are true. I believe that it is when we can truthfully say that we hold all of them that we can expect the act of declaring Christ's victory over our circumstances to bring about the transformations that we are praying for. Imagine a tub of balloons: not ordinary balloons that any sharp point will destroy, but balloons made of an indestructible skin, with an infinite capacity for expansion. God's balloons. We are all given this tub of balloons: they are all the promises of God that are Yes and Amen in Jesus. We are also given the breath to blow into them: the breath of His own Holy Spirit. When our lives are full of faith, virtue, knowledge, self-control, perseverance, godliness, brotherly kindness and love, these fill the balloon that God has led us to and it becomes active in our lives. (Is this sounding familiar? The word, and the Spirit . . .) When they are not – when, as Peter says, we are being short-sighted unto blindness – we are just flapping around a limp piece of rubber that makes the devil laugh and the Lord weep. The Lord would weep because it makes the world switch off: Jesus told us that it would be by our love that the world would see that we are His disciples, but what unbelievers see so often in the Church is people who are barren and unfruitful in their knowledge of Him, declaring His words without revealing Him in their lives.

A recent event gave me a dramatic illustration of the relationship between holding those keys and seeing God work in my situation. It was a trivial thing: I had lost my cell phone. I had prayed, but to no avail. It was morning, about 9.30, and I hadn't yet had a quiet time, so I abandoned the hunt for my phone and sat down to spend some time with the Lord. I was reading 1 Peter 3, and was arrested by verse 7, which exhorts husbands to dwell with their wives in a manner that expresses love and understanding so that "their prayers may not be hindered". As I read this verse I felt convicted that this had not been the case with me in a situation that was current at the time. Probably half, if not more, of those keys were missing from my bunch. I repented from the heart. Within seconds, someone called me on my cell phone and I heard it ringing from the other side of the house, in a room where I don't usually leave it, and which had been out of earshot when I had tried calling it earlier.

As I have said, this was hardly a life-changing circumstance, but it was one that God used in a way that I will not forget: the moment my life was in line with the word, there was the answer to my prayer. I walked through that abundant, wide-open entrance into the Kingdom and picked up my phone. It could almost have been the Lord on the line.

We learn from the apostle Peter that God's "exceedingly great and precious promises" have been given to us so that we can be "partakers of the divine nature" (2 Pet. 1:4). When Peter writes these words, he tells us that he is about to "put off his tent" – he knows that the prophecy given to him by Jesus Himself regarding the end of his life was about to be fulfilled. He is writing his last words to the Church. His concern – and he tells us this three times in the opening chapter of this second letter – is that we should be reminded, above everything else, of "these things", even though, as he says to his readers, he knows we are established in the truth of the gospel. And what is at the heart of "these things" that he so urgently wants to impart to the Church? That only as we are diligent to embrace in our own lives the character of our Saviour that our declarations of faith bring the promises of Heaven to fulfilment on Earth.

When we remember that Peter was standing right there when Jesus commanded His disciples to teach us everything He had commanded them during His Galilee ministry, and we put this in the context of Peter writing what he knows to be his last words on Earth, the importance of these "keys to the Kingdom" cannot be underestimated. So Gideon told his army to arise, because the Lord had given them the victory over the Midianites. He believed the promise, and he declared it from a place of worship and submission to God's purpose. We, the Church, need to be in this place ourselves when we make our own declarations of faith. We need to arise and wake up to the keys that God has given us if we are going to expect the word of God to become living and active in our lives and to see the darkness flee before the light.

Bible references

Judges 7:15
2 Corinthians 10:4
Psalm 2:7
Job 22:28
Hebrews 4:2
Matthew 6:33
2 Peter 1:5-11
John 10:9
Matthew 16:19
Hebrews 6:12
1 Peter 3:7
2 Peter 1:4

Chapter Seventeen
Light in the Darkness

Gideon's victory came when the army smashed their jars and light shone in the darkness. The treasure in our own earthen jars is Christ in us. For Him to shine out of our lives, our jars, too, need to be broken.

The Church is called to be light in the darkness. We know that Jesus is the Light of the World, and that those who walk in darkness will see a great light; we are exhorted to walk in the light; that we, too, are the light of the world, that our light should shine for all to see and not be hidden away, that we are to shine like stars in a crooked and perverse generation, and much more. Gideon's exhortation to arise has many echoes, but in the context of the verses that immediately follow in Judges 7, there are two that spring to mind immediately. Paul writes (Eph. 5:14 NIV): "Wake up sleeper, rise from the dead, and Christ will shine on you", and the wonderful passage in Isaiah 60 begins in a very similar tone: "Arise, shine, for your light has come, and the glory of the LORD rises upon you" (Isa. 60:1).

We have already alluded to the great now/not yet tension in scripture. Peter writes that "we have the prophetic word confirmed, which you do well to heed as a light that shines in a dark place, until the day dawns and the morning star rises in your hearts" (2 Pet. 1:19); yet if the Church is to be seen as the source of the light of Christ, it is the light that we walk in now that the world will see, not the greater light that is to come when the morning star is fully visible over the horizon. Although Peter writes of a time in the future when "the morning star rises in [our] hearts", that same Morning Star, the spirit of Christ, is in our hearts already. If the story of Gideon is given to us as a pattern for how to walk in the victory that Christ has made our own, we will see this principle at work at the point where the Midianites are first put to flight. The next verses show that this is exactly what happens. The light does come, and the darkness is put to flight. What we can learn is how this is brought about.

> "Then he divided the three hundred men *into* three companies, and he put a trumpet into every man's hand, with empty pitchers, and torches inside the pitchers."
>
> (Judg. 7:16)

We don't read about any weapons; all we know is that they went into battle with trumpets in one hand and their jars of light in the other, so whatever else they may have been carrying isn't relevant to the story, which is that they blew their trumpets and broke the jars, shouted, "A Sword for the LORD and for Gideon" (Judg. 7:20 NIV), and all the men in the enemy camp set upon each other and fled, with a suddenly swollen army of Israelites from Naphtali, Asher and Manasseh in hot pursuit. I hope that by now we all understand the significance of the trumpets, but why the torches in the jars?

Broken vessels

Arise, shine, your light has come. The light, the Morning Star, is in our hearts. Paul actually tells us (2 Cor. 4:7) that we "have this treasure in earthen vessels". What is our treasure, if not the light that we carry, Christ in us, the hope of glory? And we reveal that light when the vessel is broken.

Picture the scene again. Verse 19 tells us that Gideon had one hundred men with him at the outpost of the camp. The remaining two hundred were divided up into two other companies – small groups of one hundred warriors. The enemy was close, and their numbers countless. It was the middle watch of the night: the time when the memory of past daylight and the hope of dawn are both the furthest away. These were small churches, not congregations of thousands; but these were the ones who lapped the water and were full of the Holy Spirit. They were the ones who knew that they did not have a spirit of fear (2 Tim. 1:7), but of love, power and a sound mind. They were united in a single purpose, which was to obey the command of their leader. Gideon's command was simple:

> "Look at me and do likewise; watch, and when I come to the edge of the camp you shall do as I do".

Here Gideon demonstrates a model of leadership which Paul echoes in his letter to the young Christians at Corinth: "Imitate me, just as I also imitate Christ" (1 Cor. 11:1). Gideon had led his men to the outpost of the camp, just as the enemy had posted the watch, and here they blew their trumpets, broke their jars, revealed the light and proclaimed the name of the Lord and his commander. Gideon and his company took the lead, and all around the camp the army followed in unity and light blazed from broken vessels.

It was in brokenness that Paul imitated Christ, knowing (2 Cor. 12:10) that it is only in his weakness that he is strong: "Therefore I take pleasure in infirmities, in reproaches, in needs, in persecutions, in distresses, for Christ's sake. For when I am weak, then I am strong." Again we see that leadership in the army of the Lord does not follow the pattern of the world, but of the one who humbled himself to the point of death on the cross (Phil. 2:8). The spirit of the world is competition; the spirit of the Kingdom is unity. As one man the three companies posted around the camp blew their trumpets and broke their jars. The spirit of the world is domination, whereas the spirit of the Kingdom, as expounded by Peter in his first letter, is that we submit to one another (1 Pet. 2): spouse to spouse, citizen to ruler, brother to brother.

Jesus came not to be served, but to serve. With our jars broken all our markings of rank, our decorations of status and the adornments of the world have disappeared, and we are free to follow the one who washed His disciples' feet. A light set on a hill cannot be hidden – unless it is locked within a clay jar of the flesh. There was no individualism on that hillside when Gideon blew his trumpet, but 300 spiritual men, free from the bounds of self, ready to follow the call and glorify the Lord. There was no fear there, as, in the words of the 2016 film *The Revenant*, they had "already died". God had prepared a perfect storm for the enemy in the valley, and His eyes are on the Church today as He waits to release it again.

We must not hide our weaknesses – from others, or ourselves. The jar conceals all manner of darkness as well as the light. Yet in this Kingdom of light, even the sin in our lives can be transformed when brought into the illumination of Christ. Paul writes (Eph. 5:13 NIV), "Everything exposed by the light becomes visible – and everything that is illuminated becomes a light." The transforming power of the Holy Spirit can even turn our darkness against the enemy who put it there: sorrow to joy, mourning to dancing, fear to hope, sin to salvation. What comes to the light becomes light. Our most powerful weapons against the enemy are the areas of our lives that once were broken and now are made whole.

Amazing grace

Many are the stories of lives transformed by the light of Christ who have gone on to bring light to others who dwell in the same place of darkness that they inhabited themselves. One such story is that of John Newton, who wrote the immortal words "Amazing Grace, how sweet the sound, that saved a wretch like me."

It is well-documented that Newton was a licentious slave-trader at the time of his conversion, which happened when he cried out to God during a terrible storm off the Irish coast. There was a hole in the hull of the ship, and it was sinking. When Newton prayed, some of the cargo in the ship shifted as it rocked in the waves, and blocked the hole that was shipping water. The vessel drifted into shore, and Newton and the rest of the crew were saved. Although Newton marks this as the moment of his conversion to Christianity, he later wrote that he could not consider himself "to have been a believer in the full sense of the word, until a considerable time afterwards".

Many of us have come to Christ while our ship has been going down in the storm. At that moment He has made us whole spiritually, and has lit his lamp in our hearts. Yet it might take many years before we live out of that wholeness. It can take many years before we finally realise that our protection and our security is not in the jar, but the light itself that it contains. Newton's shipwreck was in 1748. In 1754 he retired from the slave trade and was ordained as an Anglican minister, writing 280 hymns to accompany his services, but he continued to invest in the slave trade. Only in 1788 did he finally renounce the slave trade with the publication of a pamphlet in which he described the horrific conditions in which the slaves were transported. He wrote at the time: "It will always be a subject of humiliating reflection to me, that I was once an active instrument in a business at which my heart now shudders." Newton wrote the words of "Amazing Grace" in 1772, but it took him forty years to finally smash his jar. When he did, his pamphlet was so popular that it was reprinted many times, and circulated to every Member of Parliament. In September 1807, the slave trade was eventually abolished under William Wilberforce. Newton died in December of the same year.

That place of being a "believer in the full sense of the word", as Newton called it, is on the hillside with the 300, jar smashed and light revealed. Where are we? Are we still drifting in the storm, but safe at least in the knowledge that we are no longer going to sink because Christ has made us whole? Are we building our new lives, even building our ministries and writing beautiful words, but still clinging onto our jars and all that they represent? Or are we ready to break them and live to see history made?

Bible references

Ephesians 5:14

Isaiah 60:1

2 Peter 1:19

Judges 7:16

Judges 7:20

2 Corinthians 4:7

2 Timothy 1:7

1 Corinthians 11:1

2 Corinthians 12:10

Philippians 2:8

1 Peter 2

Ephesians 5:13

Chapter Eighteen
Standing

Like Moses who stood still and saw the salvation of his God, Gideon and the 300 stood on the mountain while God did the work in the enemy camp. For us today, to "stand on the word" we need to be filled with the word; to stand in God's armour we need to be wearing it all; and to stand against the enemy we need to stand together.

"And every man stood in his place all around the camp; and the whole army ran and cried out and fled" (Judg. 7:21). "Look at them run!" said Gideon. "After them quickly! God is with us!" And the 300 charged down the hill with Gideon at their head.

If that had happened next, we can be certain that there would be no story of victory for our edification. But how easy it would have been for Gideon and his men to be caught up in the enthusiasm of the moment as they saw God's hand at work, and run down the mountain to finish the job. "Thank you, Lord – we can do the rest!" As I keep saying – how easy it is to imitate the "foolish Galatians" and let the flesh take over from the Spirit.

Having begun in the Spirit, the 300 continued in the Spirit: they stood where they were while God did the work. Some of them may even have known the words of Moses at the edge of the Red Sea, when he exhorted the Israelites to "stand still and see the salvation of the LORD" (Exod. 14:13). If they did, they would have experienced the thrill of faith rising as the truth of God's word was enacted before their eyes. But whether or not they knew of this glorious precedent, they didn't leave their positions and go charging down the mountain; instead they all stood in their places around the camp.

In his famous commentary on Paul's letter to the Ephesians, Watchman Nee summarises the three stances of faith under the headings "Sit, Walk, Stand". Paul teaches that we cannot begin our journey in Christ unless we start from a position of knowing that Jesus did everything, but everything, for us at Calvary. There is not a sin uncovered, not a need unmet that God hasn't provided for in the fullness of His grace, and we, the Church, are already seated with Christ in heavenly places. From this position, and this position only, we begin to learn to "walk in the Spirit". Finally, having understood our position in Christ and learnt how to walk with Him; and only then, "having done all", clothed in the full armour of God, do we stand against the armies of the evil one (Eph. 6:10-18).

When Jesus was crucified, the enemy was routed. As the Midianites fled, each of the 300 men "stood in his place". They had walked, and now God was doing the work. So how do we stand, and where? What do we do while we are standing?

In church parlance, we use the phrase "standing on the word of God". We won't find it in scripture, but we all know what it means. We believe God has spoken about a circumstance, and we say, "God's word is true; the circumstances I see are subject to the word of God, and therefore the word of God will prevail." We have looked in a previous chapter at the difference between "claiming" any word out of scripture that seems to be relevant to our situation – picking a sentence or two out of the entire Logos, as it were – and receiving a word spoken by God into that moment in our lives – the *Rhema* word. When the Holy Spirit speaks a scripture into our heart we can stand in faith on what He has said, but I believe that hunting, by our own efforts, through the Bible or through a book of promises, to see what might be written there for today's difficulties is likely to lead to disappointment and broken dreams. The first seems to me to be living faith; the second seems more like dead religion. I believe we must always put our trust in what we know the Holy Spirit has said to us personally, as we walk with Him, step by step, through our lives. It's not enough to read the book: we must listen to the Author. Jesus Himself summed up the difference (John 5:39-40) when He told the Pharisees: "You search the Scriptures, for in them you think you have eternal life; and these are they which testify of Me. But you are not willing to come to Me that you may have life." Let us not be deceived by the same religious spirits as they were.

I want to change the preposition from "on" to "in". Can we stand "in" the word? As Ezekiel stood in the river, up to his ankles, then up to his knees, up to his waist and finally until it was so deep he could no longer stand without being submerged, can we be equally immersed in the word of God?

I was at a life group (small group/cell group/house group – whatever your brand) not long ago, and I simply wasn't participating: I was physically uncomfortable because the room was particularly hot and stuffy, and my spirit was completely closed down. I had no sense of the presence of God, no quickening from the Holy Spirit about anything, and on top of that no particular desire to do anything about the situation. What I actually wanted to do was to leave the room and go for a walk down the street in the evening sunshine. What I did not want to do was sit where I was on that sofa and pretend that I was joining in prayers that were just bouncing off me. I managed not to leave the room – that would have caused consternation and disrupted everyone's prayers – but I just got out of my seat and moved to the other end of the room, explaining briefly that my legs were uncomfortable and I needed to stand up and move around for a while.

I have described this context in some detail because it shows that I clearly was not "in a good place" spiritually at that moment. But more important, it also shows that we do not have to be "in a good place" for the Holy Spirit to speak to us and get our attention.

While I was standing there, thinking I still didn't particularly want to go and sit down again, a very clear picture came into my mind. So unexpected, with my state at that moment so carnal and unreceptive, that I didn't realise straight away that the Lord was speaking to me. It was a picture of a human silhouette filled with words and phrases, in different styles and typefaces and at different angles to each other, but completely filling the human shape. It looked as though they all belonged to longer sentences that had been cut out by the shape of the silhouette, just as if it were a gingerbread man pastry cutter. I couldn't read any of the words, but the sense of the picture became clear as I considered it: we need to be completely filled with the word of God.

Let's stop and think a minute about truth. Jesus is the way, the truth and the light. We know that God's word is truth. We know, because

Jesus, the truth, tells us, that we bring judgement on ourselves for every "idle word" we speak. We know that we should let no corrupt word proceed from our mouths, but only that which is good for necessary edification. We know that the body of Christ is built up ("edified") as we speak the truth in love to one another. These are all well-known New Testament precepts. And they point to one inescapable fact: we have a stark choice between building one another up by speaking the truth in love, or bringing judgement on ourselves by letting corrupt, idle words come out of our mouths. And if the truth is always to be found in Jesus and His words, we find the significance of that gingerbread-man picture: there is no room in our lives for anything that does not have its source in the living word of God; every other word is corrupt, idle and ultimately a lie. The word of God must fill us and flow through us. If we are to live as victorious warriors for Christ we need to stand fully in it, immersed in it; not just on it.

Needless to say, the entire Bible was not printed across that silhouette: I had the impression that the words and phrases were fluid and would change – the point was that they filled the shape. We are told that God would write His word on our hearts. I think we can believe that the Holy Spirit will so guide us that the scriptures He wants to write on our hearts are ones that will speak into the situations He is taking us through. Or to turn it round – He will take us through situations through which He can write on our hearts the scriptures He has for us at any given time. A good teacher always has his lessons prepared. The works that have been prepared for us to walk in (Eph. 2:10) are lessons for our own lives as well as testimony for others. Jesus is the Good Teacher: let us use the lessons He has prepared for us to learn how to stand in, and be filled with, His word.

So why, if I know this, do I find it so difficult to do? Why, even in the last couple of hours, have I spoken stuff that is not edifying, was not spoken in love, and was, in some way, not true?

The full armour

A key to this can be found in that most famous section on "standing" referred to above: Ephesians 6:10-18. Clothed in the full armour of God, we stand against the wiles of the evil one. Having "done all", we are to stand. Notice that we are exhorted, twice, to put on the FULL armour, just like that silhouette was FULL of the word of God. We can leave no gaps, no chinks. Many believers make a regular practice of "putting on the armour", going through a process of reading or reciting the Ephesians 6 verses as a declaration of preparedness for battle. Personally, I don't think those verses were ever meant for that purpose. Speaking out the words "breastplate of righteousness", "helmet of salvation", "shoes of the gospel of peace", or the other items in Paul's armoury doesn't equip us to stand against the forces of evil, unless they are used as a prompt to remind us that we are the righteousness of God in Christ, that we have the mind of Christ, or that He will keep us in perfect peace if our minds are stayed on Him, and if we take the time to repent and seek restoration in any of those areas that are wanting. Because the armour is a representation of the fullness of Christ, we aren't supposed to keep putting it on – we are never meant to take it off. If we are missing any of it – losing God's peace, straying from the truth, letting our minds wander from the joy of our salvation, or letting any other piece of the armour drop – we are immediately vulnerable to the enemy, and God's word will not be flowing through us in power. And if God's word isn't filling us, other words, from the flesh or the devil, will be. They won't be words to stand on.

So Paul's reminder on standing in the fullness of Christ also has specific relevance to "standing on the word". When we are fully submitted to and filled with the Spirit of God, the word will be living and active in us and will accomplish the purpose of the One who sent it. But this scripture also reveals another reason why we must always take up the whole armour of God, and not just some of it. The battle that we wage against the evil forces in heavenly realms is fought in prayer. While we stand in that armour, Paul tells us that we are to be "praying always with all prayer and supplication in the Spirit, being watchful to this end with all perseverance and supplication for all the saints – and for me, that utterance may be given to me, that I may open my mouth boldly to make known the mystery of the gospel" (vs.18-19). We wear the armour, and we pray for the advance of the Kingdom. We know from the apostle James that "the effective fervent prayer of a righteous man avails much" (Jas. 5:16). How do we make sure that our prayers are fervent and effective? By standing in the fullness of the armour of God. If, when we pray, we are standing at the heart of all that is meant by God's truth, righteousness, and peace, His faith (remember it's the faith "of God"), His salvation and His word, what indeed can stand against us? "Neither death nor life, nor angels nor principalities nor powers, nor things present nor things to come, nor height nor depth, nor any other created thing" (Rom. 8:38-39). The purpose of the armour is not just to protect us from the enemy; it is to make our prayers effective.

Holding fast the Word of Life

One of my favourite scriptures, one that I keep quoting because I think it beautifully defines our calling and mission as God's people, is Paul's instruction to the Philippians to "Do all things without complaining and disputing, that you may become blameless and harmless, children of God without fault in the midst of a crooked and perverse generation, among whom you shine as lights in the world, holding fast the word of life" (Phil. 2:14-16).

Again, this is the complete package. We cannot hold fast (stand on) the word of life unless we shine as lights in the world, and we cannot shine if our ways (how we do all things) are not blameless and harmless – fully submitted to Christ. The instruction to do all things without complaining or disputing goes deeper than just not "making a fuss"; it touches our deepest emotional and intellectual states. "Complaining" refers to murmuring – an unexpressed resentment, secret mutterings. We only have two contexts for the word in the NT: one is in Acts 6, when the dispute arose about caring for the widows in the Church; the other is in John 7:2, when some said Jesus was good, while others said He was a deceiver. It describes words that bring division, spoken covertly against leadership (Acts 6) and Jesus himself (John 7). It would aptly describe the murmurings of the Israelites against Moses as he led them through the desert. These complaints are the rebellious mutterings of an unsubmitted heart, and we must guard against them if we are to hold fast the word of life.

While "complaining" refers more to a heart attitude, "disputing" is something that takes place in the mind. The Greek word is *dialogismos*, and refers to debate, or argument, where two sides to a case are being presented. It is the root, clearly enough, of the word "dialogue". It suggests questioning, deliberation, doubt, reasoning with oneself. Where there is disputing there is unbelief. Where disputing is absent, faith abounds. Where there is complaining, self rises up; where complaining is absent, love can rule.

There is a requirement on us if we are to be people who stand in faith and manifest the shining light of God's word in the darkness of this world: all our actions ("do everything") must stem from wholehearted and unquestioning obedience to the Holy Spirit, with every unbelieving thought taken captive to the obedience of Christ; and from a submitted heart where every selfish agenda is nailed to the cross.

The sword of division

We live in the end-time world that Jesus prophesied, where family members are divided against one another, where nations war and where faction rises against faction. Jesus told us that

He didn't come to bring peace, but a sword; and we see that sword brandished on a daily basis as Christians are murdered and persecuted for their faith. As the darkness around us deepens, so the light must become more intense; a beacon for the lost where they can find salvation. In a world where morality is defined by fifty shades of grey, the light of the gospel appears to many as just another choice, another tint in the spectrum; but as grey turns to black the light of the Kingdom will become ever more separate from the shadows, and will be seen from afar by everyone who seeks. In those days, we are told, the Lord will tell us what to speak; and when He does we know that His word will go out in power. But against this backdrop the enemy has another plan: not just to chop us down, as much as he delights in doing so, but to divide us from within.

There will always be denominations, because ultimately there are as many expressions of faith as there are individual Christians. But these are also the days of the internet, where every trumpeting voice, whether for good or for evil, has an echo-chamber; every lone wolf finds a pack, and every dissenter has an audience. And in this environment the enemy points to the sword of division and offers it to the Church. In the world we can expect nation to rise against nation, but Jesus has established His Church to manifest a different spirit. Yet Christian writers and church leaders take to their blogs and websites to denounce the theology of brothers and sisters in the name of "contending for the faith", wise in their own opinions, denying the very spirit of the faith they profess so ardently, and forgetting what Paul said to the Philippians, which was "in lowliness of mind" to "let each esteem others better than himself" (Phil. 2:3). There is only one place where we will see the enemy routed, and that is standing together with Gideon in his camp high up the mountainside. Before He went to the cross, Jesus prayed that we would all be one. However many are standing together in that place, affirming, loving and finding Jesus in one another – and we know that the Commander of our army doesn't count heads – they will be the ones who shine and from whom the blessings will flow. Whoever runs down the hill brandishing a sword risks ultimately being destroyed by it.

Bible references

Judges 7:21

Exodus 14:13

Ephesians 6:10-18

John 5:39-40

Ephesians 2:10

James 5:16

Romans 8:38-39

Philippians 2:14-16

Philippians 2:3

Chapter Nineteen
Pressing On

By his humble response to the complaints of the men of Ephraim, Gideon was able to keep them onside and hunt down the princes of Midian. Similarly we must keep our relationships right, and also walk in the opposite spirit to the world, if we are going to chase down the principalities and powers who seek to bring destruction into our midst.

T he end of Gideon's story (Judg. 8:12-35) anticipates in one respect the greatest victory of all: the victory of Jesus at Calvary. Although Jesus defeated the enemy once and for all, the Church is still engaged in battle. When the trumpets were blown the Midianites were defeated, but it wasn't until their princes and kings were dead that the campaign was over and the land had rest. Part of the story tells how Gideon punished the men of Penuel and Succoth because they would not support him by feeding his men. This seems like a brutal account that just serves to remind us how far removed were the Old Testament ways from the grace of today. But while our manner may not be as harsh, are there times when our hearts and minds are equally closed to other churches and ministries whose vision we do not share? Whoever passes through our "city" in pursuit of our common enemy, God wants us to support and love them – give them bread – whether or not we are standing with them in faith for their objectives. As we saw in the last chapter, there is ultimately no position where we can stand in victory outside of complete John 17 unity: this account of division in the tribes of Israel serves to point us to the goal we must pursue.

We pursue unity, therefore, because where there is division there is also destruction. But there are two other pursuits that are central to the life of the Kingdom warrior: the one described in the narrative of Judges 8, which is the pursuit of the kings and princes of the enemy; and the other, the opposite, which is the pursuit described by Paul in Philippians 3: the pursuit of our relationship with Jesus. We will consider that, the greatest pursuit of all, in the next chapter.

The end of Judges 7 tells us how the men of Ephraim pursued the armies of Midian and brought the heads of their princes, Oreb and Zeeb, to Gideon on the far side of the Jordan. They were angry that Gideon had not called on them earlier – whether for the glory or the spoils of victory is not revealed – but Gideon's response anticipates an important New Testament principle. He says to them: "'God has delivered into your hands the princes of Midian, Oreb and Zeeb. And what was I able to do in comparison with you?' Then their anger toward him subsided when he said that" (Judg. 8:3).

To prefer one another is an expression of Kingdom love. Our relationships with God and with one another are the most important thing in our lives, but they can be threatened so easily. Whenever they break down we either have to take the time and energy to work on their restoration, or we have to accept that the enemy has won a battle, destroyed a valuable part of our lives, and brought down a channel through which God's kingdom-building love can now no longer be extended. When they do break down, it is usually because we are in some way preferring ourselves and not one another. We are valuing our own agenda or self-justification more than we are valuing our relationship. If Gideon had felt his leadership threatened here, he could have given the men of Ephraim any number of reasons why he hadn't needed their help. They would all have been justified, but they all would have conveyed the message that he knew what he was doing because he was the one whom God had chosen to lead this campaign, and it was his men, not them, who had clearly been chosen for the task. Instead, he kept his eyes on his relationships and not on his ego, and through his humble response Gideon kept the men of Ephraim onside and was able to take the battle to the next level, which was the pursuit and capture of the kings. If he had alienated them through any kind of arrogant or imperious reaction to their complaint he may have had an uprising on his hands that would have distracted him from the task in hand. The kings of Midian could have regrouped, and the story could have had a very different outcome. But as it was he was able to keep his focus on the one thing that was important, which was to hunt down Zebah and Zalmunnah, the kings of Midian.

Another lesson for the Church that the Holy Spirit has written into this account is that our battle is against "the rulers of the darkness of this age" (Eph. 6:12). While we read (vs.10-12) that the entire army of Midian was being routed, it was their kings that Gideon was hunting down. Paul referred to "principalities", "powers", "rulers" and "spiritual wickedness in high places". They haven't gone away since the answers to Daniel's prayers were delayed by the Prince of Persia (Dan. 10:13). Who are they? How do they operate? How do we fight them? And what, for example, is the Prince of Persia doing today? (Iran's hatred of Israel may be a clue . . .)

I think we have to be careful not to be too dogmatic about how we understand Paul's terminology here. Are the princes of Persia and Grecia referred to in Daniel 10 principalities, powers or rulers, for example? The term "principality" (*archē*) refers to one who is first in rank, or an originator. We have the word "arch", as in archetype, or arch-rival, or architect among other derivations. A principality is clearly "up there" in the demonic hierarchy. The word "power" (*exousia*) means authority or strength. It can mean the power that is exercised by choice: spiritual beings who have chosen evil over good, and made a decision to align themselves with Satan. This could refer to the entire cohort of "one third of the stars of heaven" that fell in the rebellion, if indeed this is what the verse in Revelation 12:4 is describing. A ruler (*kosmokratōr*) is a demonic lord, clearly a demon of some rank, but possibly less than a principality. But the term that is not open to interpretation is High Places. *Epouranios* means heavenly, not earthly. Exactly what the relationship between these different beings is we are not told, but what we are told is everything that we need to know: they exist in the spiritual dimension, they have identities, they influence what goes on around us, and, like Gideon, we have to go after them.

We learn from Judges 2:21 – 3:3 that the Lord stopped driving out the nations before His people, as He had in the time of Joshua, because He wanted to test their obedience so that they might be "taught to know war" (Judg. 3:2). The Canaanites and other tribes were left in the land "that He might test Israel by them, to know whether they would obey the commandments of the LORD, which He had commanded their fathers by the hand of Moses" (Judg. 3:4). What scripture seems to tell us here is not so much that God wanted His children to have to fight, but that knowing war would teach them to obey His commandments. In obedience to Him they would find deliverance from their enemies, but in rebellion they would experience defeat.

At the cross, Jesus fulfilled the Law on our behalf, and has left us with just one command: that we love one another. He tells us (Judg. 3:3) that we are His friends if we obey His commandments. We can ask the Holy Spirit to reveal which spiritual forces of wickedness we are engaging with at any given time, but central to any battle must be obedience to the command to love one another. We know that our salvation is secure because we are clothed with the righteousness of Jesus Christ, and nothing can come between us and the love of our God. We know that our names are written in the Book of Life. But we cannot walk in the Spirit unless we are walking in and showing His love, because this is what is poured into our hearts by the Spirit. And if we are not walking in the Spirit we are not wearing God's armour, and we are going to get hit. Nothing has changed. Before we go chasing after demons, we must make sure our love for one another is complete.

So, assuming that our relationships are right with God, how do we pursue the Zeba and Zalmunna that want to rule the circumstances around us?

Jesus gave us the strategy, and Luke recorded it in chapter 10 verse 3 of his gospel: "I send you out as lambs among wolves."

He spells it out in the Sermon on the Mount: if someone wants to take our tunic, we give him our cloak as well. We walk two miles with the person who compels us to walk one. We love our enemies. We pray for those who abuse and mistreat us. Whatever spirit of wickedness is prevailing in our circumstances, our community or our region, we move against it by acting in the opposite spirit. This is the battle strategy of grace. St Francis of Assisi, the man who exhorted us to "share the gospel by all means possible, and if necessary use words", expressed it in his famous prayer:

Lord, make me an instrument of Your peace. Where there is hatred, let me sow love; where there is injury, pardon; where there is doubt, faith; where there is despair, hope; where there is darkness, light; where there is sadness, joy.

O, Divine Master, grant that I may not so much seek to be consoled as to console; to be understood as to understand; to be loved as to love; For it is in giving that we receive; it is in pardoning that we are pardoned; it is in dying that we are born again to eternal life.

We don't build the Church of Christ using the tools of the enemy, but with the gifts of grace. Demons won't flee just because we shout at them in the name of Jesus, but when they see that His light really is coming to drive out their darkness. Central to this light, and contrary to so much that runs amok in the darkness, is forgiveness. If we want to be effective in our pursuit of Zeba and

Zalmunna, it is essential that we pass the test that Paul put to the Corinthians:

> "Another reason I wrote you was to see if you would stand the test and be obedient in everything. Anyone you forgive, I also forgive. And what I have forgiven – if there was anything to forgive – I have forgiven in the sight of Christ for your sake, in order that Satan might not outwit us. For we are not unaware of his schemes."
>
> (2 Cor. 2:9-11 NIV)

At the very core of our salvation is the full and free forgiveness granted at the cross to all who believe. At the core of Satan's strategy is to prevent the message of that forgiveness from spreading on Earth, and to dilute, distort and discredit it in those hearts where it has been received. He is called the "accuser of the brethren" (1 Tim. 4:13), and he is described in the Book of Revelation as the one who accused them (the brethren) day and night before God. Many of Satan's "schemes", therefore, depend on blame, revenge, judgement and similar unforgiving attitudes of the heart. We cannot expect to be effective against enemy forces if we carry his weapons around with us. Just as God tests the obedience of the Israelites in the time of the judges, He tests ours today. We will not know His victory in our lives unless we obey the command we have received, which is to forgive those who trespass against us. When we forgive, we are like God; when we don't, we are like the enemy. And Paul tells us that we "wrestle" with these powers of darkness: it is not an occasional skirmish, but full-on, in-your-face engagement. If we hold unforgiveness in our hearts, we will find ourselves lying on the mat with our arm twisted behind our backs and a demon sitting on our shoulders as we cry out for deliverance that doesn't come.

The wrestling match

I believe that this "wrestling" is the norm in our personal lives. We know that the flesh is weak, because Jesus told us Himself, and it is the flesh that the enemy seeks to lay hold of and grapple with in order to lead us astray from our spiritual walk. But just as any of the powers of darkness are stronger than our fleshly will and will wrestle us to the ground, so we are stronger in Christ than any of the defeated powers of darkness. When we conform to Christ's death, we also conform to His victorious resurrection (Phil. 3:10): every time we die to self; every time we "present [our] bodies as a living sacrifice" (Rom. 12:1), the enemy that would pull us down is faced with a spirit man or woman who is seated with Christ in heavenly places, and the battle is over. We need to know that there is often more going on than physical and emotional reactions to situations. Anne and I often host small group at our house, and I will lead worship. When I arrive home from work at between 6.30 and 7.00 p.m. what I want to do is have my dinner then sit and not do much else for a while: maybe watch some TV, read a book or listen to some music. I am tired and hungry, and have no desire to go prayerfully through the worship book, pick up my guitar, and prepare something for 8.00 p.m. While my spirit man is longing for fellowship with Father and my brothers and sisters, the enemy is grappling with my flesh and trying to pull me away. Thank God for the victory we have in Christ!

Every time we choose the Spirit over the flesh we are winning a wrestling match; we are chasing after Zeba and Zalmunna. Paul writes of renewing the mind (Rom. 12:2) in the context of presenting our bodies as a living sacrifice. We know the personal enemies that we wrestle with. We know, because it is written (Jas. 4:7), that when we resist the devil, he will flee. If I have a problem with laziness, which I do, I face that particular wrestling match on a daily, if not hourly basis. "Don't bother to put that away – it doesn't matter for now." "Leave that – you can do it later." The book of Proverbs tell us that the vineyard of a lazy man is full of briars and nettles and its walls are broken down (Prov. 24:30-31). I can leave those clothes lying on the floor and let the nettles grow, or I can face that enemy, go after him, and work on building my wall. With every battle that we win, we renew our minds just a little more.

The spirit of mammon

This pursuit extends beyond our personal lives. The essence of the Sermon on the Mount is this: "You have heard . . . but I tell you . . ." The world and the spirits that Satan would have controlling it gives us one message, but the Kingdom of God and the King on the throne point us in the opposite direction. This is as apparent as anywhere in the world of business, where the prevailing spirits of self-interest, suspicion and competition run contrary to the ethos of the Kingdom. Mammon, whom we cannot serve at the same time as serving God, is a name of Aramaic origin meaning wealth or treasure personified, and with that personification comes a sense of strutting confidence. Mammon, as a man, would be someone who is the very figure of wealth, supremely confident in his power to achieve anything he wants, and totally secure in the fortune he has amassed. Mammon would behave and think like somebody who believes he owns the world and is blind to any other possibility. Protecting and furthering his interests are his first and final thoughts, and all his systems are designed to further those ends. He will of course walk by sight and not by faith, and he will walk after the flesh and not after the spirit. For Mammon, read the world economic system and the organisations that support it.

Jesus is Lord of all, however. While we cannot serve Him at the same time as serving Mammon, we can serve Him when working in the same system as those who do. We can be in it, but not of it. The calling of the Christian business is to reveal the glory and goodness of God and to further His purposes where the shadow of Mammon falls by being different from those who operate under it. We recently needed to employ another member of staff for our warehouse. To ensure that the right person is selected for the job, the usual procedure in the world of employment is to advertise, interview, then appoint. The number of interviewees will depend on the number of applicants. We had over 100 applicants to sift through. Many of them looked like they would suit the job. When we were interviewing the second person we invited, who on paper was far from the best candidate, the Holy Spirit said to Anne, "He's the one." Working by faith and not by sight, we employed him. What we didn't know, and what we only found out a few days later as we were chatting to him, was that he was a man who had seen his life as going nowhere and had cried out to God for a better job. God is at work in this person's life, and was giving us the opportunity to be involved. What a privilege we would have missed if we had gone through the accepted procedure and picked the strongest candidate: we would have picked Eliab and missed David. When we operate in the opposite spirit to the world we are pursuing Zeba and Zalmunna in victory instead of being driven along by them in defeat.

Our cities are places where sin is rampant and crime is rife, and where it would seem that the devil is having his way. None more so, probably, than Los Angeles, where to many people Hollywood is the home of the gods. If we were looking for somewhere that stood for family values, we would not pick Los Angeles from any list. But Los Angeles was founded by a group of Christian families, and God has not abandoned His purposes there. In his book *Translating God*, Shawn Bolz tells of how God called him over many years to Los Angeles. The advice from Christian friends and colleagues around him was "Don't go there!", but he followed the insistent prompting of the Spirit to start a church based on Christian family values in that place. He knew nothing of the history of its foundation, but he was led supernaturally to the very spot where that first church was built. In walking by faith and not by sight he is partnering with the Holy Spirit in completing a work that He began with a small group of Christian families many years ago.

There is a corollary to this story. In 1993 a thriving church group that I know was told by the Holy Spirit, through a prophetic word from a visiting speaker, to "Go" into their community and establish a particular ministry there, outside of the comfort zone of the church building. The word that came was: "The time is now; if you don't go now it will be twenty-five years before it will happen again." The church didn't heed the word, the flow of the Holy Spirit that had been powerful in that place until then, bringing salvation and restoration, began to dry up; people began to fall away, the congregation started to dwindle and has never returned to the strength of the time when the word to go into the community was brought. The twenty-five years is nearly up, and it seems like the Holy Spirit might be bringing people back into the congregation who could revive that work. Meanwhile, a generation has been lost. If we don't go after the Kings of Midian when God tells us to, they will come after us.

Like everything else that I have touched on in this book, there is so much more that could be written on this topic. There are ruling powers over nations and over lesser communities. Sometimes the Holy Spirit will show your church what they are and what to do about them. If we listen to the Holy Spirit and do what He says, the enemy has to lose his grip on whatever it is we are involved in, and we will walk in the works that God has prepared for us before the foundation of the world. When it comes to pursuing the enemy, the final word in the chapter is good for any other chapter in our lives: we need to walk by faith and not by sight.

Bible references

Judges 8:3

Ephesians 6:12

Daniel 10:13

Revelation 12:4

Judges 3:2

Judges 3:4

Judges 3:3

Luke 10:3

2 Corinthians 2:9-11

1 Timothy 4:13

Philippians 3:10

Romans 12:1

Romans 12:2

James 4:7

Proverbs 24:30-31

Chapter Twenty
The Golden Ephod

The ephod bore a pouch that contained the Urim and Thummim; the means by which the priest discerned the will of God. In the idol of the golden ephod that Gideon set up we see a picture of religion in the Church today, where adherence to dead forms and rituals hinder us from entering into the presence of the living Christ. Paul's injunction to the Colossians not to be deceived by "commandments and doctrines of men" was to be read also at the church at Laodicea, which, not long later, Jesus Himself would castigate in His Revelation to the apostle John as being "lukewarm".

Wherever religion has a foothold in our meetings, Jesus stands at the door and knocks – waiting for us to let Him in.

The story of Gideon ends where it began: with Israel in idolatry. After such a great victory, how could it all go wrong?

"Then Gideon made it into an ephod and set it up in his city, Ophrah. And all Israel played the harlot with it there. It became a snare to Gideon and to his house."

(Judg. 8:27)

The men of Israel had asked Gideon to rule over them, but Gideon's reply was "The Lord shall rule over you" (v.23). He asked each man to give the gold earrings from his plunder, and with the gold he cast the ephod. No small thing either: the weight of the gold earrings alone came to one thousand seven hundred shekels (somewhere in the region of 40lbs or 18kg weight), so this was not an ephod that any priest was going to wear over his priestly garments. The narrative concludes with verses 28-29: "Thus Midian was subdued before the children of Israel, so that they lifted their heads no more. And the country was quiet for forty years in the days of Gideon. Then Jerubbaal the son of Joash went and dwelt in his own house."

The logic of the English language suggests that Gideon returned to his house after the forty years. But clearly that is not the case: having said that he would not rule over the Israelites, he set up the Ephod, and that would be when he said, "That's it. Job done. I'm retiring now." We read also that he had many wives, and had seventy sons by them. Although the details aren't revealed in the story, I think it is safe to assume that he gained these wives after the battle, when he was wealthy (he would have kept a lot of the plunder) and successful; not beforehand when he was hiding in the winepress. A detail that I believe is there for our edification is that it was Gideon who won the battle, and Gideon whom the Lord honoured with forty years of peace during his lifetime, but "Jerubbaal the son of Joash" who took early retirement. The derivation of the name Gideon isn't certain, but commentaries suggests it probably means "cutter down" – one who cuts down the enemy. Jerubbaal is the name given to him by his father when he tore down the altar of Baal, and means "let Baal contend".

The point for us here is that the gifts and calling of God are without repentance. We might step aside from an office conferred on us by a church authority structure, but we don't step out of the battle to see the Kingdom of God established on Earth. We are called for life to the work of Gideon, to the pulling down – or cutting down – of strongholds; not until we draw our pension or until we go to work on Monday morning. Some commentaries suggest that Gideon refused to rule over Israel out of submission to the Hebrew understanding of Israel's identity as a theocracy, but there is no more evidence of this in the text than the possibility that he simply wanted to enjoy the rest of his life living off the spoils of his victory. Either way, the lesson for the Church is there: if we choose to sit back and stop cutting down the enemy, we do indeed "let Baal contend".

Because Baal did contend: the Israelites abandoned the Lord and made Baal – Berith their god. Abimelech, Gideon's son by a concubine in Shechem, murdered all but the youngest of Gideon's seventy sons, in order to rule over Israel himself. To achieve this he hired "worthless men", whom he paid with seventy pieces of silver. The silver came from the temple of Baal-Perith. Gideon's legacy was destroyed and darkness ruled again. Leadership in the Church can only be through anointed ministry, activated as Spirit-led warriors walk in obedience to the Lord. The warrior in Christ and child of God is Gideon; the natural man of the natural father is Jerubbaal son of Joash. The ephod and the natural man are connected: when the ephod was set up as the Lord of Israel the natural man followed his own inclinations instead of following the Lord.

We see the golden ephod in church today. We can see it wherever the liquid gold of worship is cast in the unyielding form of a set structure. So many of us mocked the "hymn-prayer" sandwich in the early days of the charismatic movement. Do we really think our chorus-word sandwich is any more Spirit-filled today? Gideon is nowhere to be seen: Jerubbaal is in his own house. He may be praying and singing spiritual songs, but he's not in the Temple of the Lord, because that place is filled with God's glory; and he's not doing battle anywhere because the spiritual atmosphere in his city is the same as it always was.

When set patterns and institutions hold sway, the golden ephod is set up, religion takes over, Gideon gives way to Jerubbaal, and the battle is lost for another generation. The fires of revival become a memorial of near-empty church buildings. As God raises up Gideon's company for the last days, He is also laying bare the golden ephods that are weakening the Church.

This is nothing new: Paul's criticism of the "foolish Galatians" was because they were succumbing to pressure from the judaizers to come under Old Covenant Law through circumcision. But I think that it is through parts of the Epistle to the Colossians that the Holy Spirit speaks to us particularly clearly about those things that can become a snare for the Church today.

The initial salutations are hardly over before Paul is establishing to the Colossians the great truths that Jesus is the "image of the invisible God", that He is "before all things, and in Him all things consist", that "in all things He may have the pre-eminence", that "it pleased *the Father that* in Him all the fullness should dwell, and by Him to reconcile all things to Himself" (including ourselves, "who once were alienated and enemies in [our] mind by wicked works"), "by Him, whether things on earth or things in heaven, having made peace through the blood of His cross" (from Col. 1:15-21). In these great sweeping verses Paul is at pains to paint a picture of the absolute majesty and divinity of the God who brought us into His own wonderful Kingdom through the agony and death of the cross. The Colossians, and the Church throughout the ages, are left in no doubt about the abject state of our natural condition, the limitless grace of the God who saves us, and the glory of the destiny of those who walk in this gift of His love. The exchange of flesh for Spirit is total, absolute, and magnificent. What God has revealed to the saints, Paul tells us, is nothing less than "the mystery which has been hidden from ages and from generation" (Col. 1:26). What is this mystery? It's the treasure we carry in those earthen vessels, the light in the jars that the 300 broke on the mountain: Christ in us, the hope of glory (v.27).

Christ in us. What a thought. This Creator God, the Head of all things, this loving, compassionate Saviour who gave His life for His enemies so they could become His friends; this Messiah prophesied over centuries: He is in us. Up to this point the Author of the Bible, the Holy Spirit, has taken great care to establish in our minds the importance of our identity "in Christ". It is in Him that we live and move (see Acts: 17:28). And now the revelation comes: this same Christ is in us. How can this make sense? It's no surprise of course: the very substance of Jesus's final prayer in Gethsemane is both "that they also may be one in Us, that the world may believe that You sent Me" (John 17:21) and "I in them, and You in Me; that they may be made perfect in one, and that the world may know that You have sent Me" (v.23). Us in Him, and Him in us: both revealing Jesus to the world.

This amazing, impossible situation, the fulfilment of which is also the deepest cry of the Saviour's heart, can only be understood in the light of one person, in many ways the opposite of the golden ephod: the person of the Holy Spirit. The ephod was an external vestment, possibly some sort of pouch, which housed the Urim and Thummim, the sacred objects used for divining the will of the Lord. The Holy Spirit lives inside us, and He guides us in our paths. The ephod was a static, dead object; the Holy Spirit is a dynamic living Being. The golden ephod was cast in worldly riches; the Holy Spirit brings us the treasures of Heaven. The Ephod could only be worn by someone of high priestly office; the Holy Spirit dwells in all believers. The ephod represents dead religion and human thinking; the Holy Spirit leads us into living worship and brings us the mind of Christ.

We know, because Jesus repeats it enough times, that the Kingdom of Heaven is "at hand". It's "near". Although there are times, both biblically and in the anecdotal canon of people's "God Stories", when people have sensed themselves being lifted vertically into heavenly places, our understanding of scripture and of the experience of Christians over the ages is that Heaven is a dimension inaccessible to mortals other than by special invitation from the Lord; it's not a place "up there". I think it's probably closer to the truth to see the finite universe as just some sort of little bubble in the infinite dimension that God inhabits. Whatever that truth is, we know that the Father and the Son are on thrones in Heaven, and the Holy Spirit is the one who is active on Earth on their behalf. Angels and demons are also active within our bubble. Part of the work of the Holy Spirit involves passing between the two dimensions: He is present both on Earth and in Heaven. We know this because Jesus tells us, in John 16:14, that He "will take of what is Mine and declare it to you". If we keep hold of the idea of a spiritual dimension and abandon the notion of spatial ones, it is much easier to grasp the idea of our born-again spirits, through the power of the Holy Spirit within us, literally being in two places at once: seated with Christ in heavenly places, and active in the earthly realm. If now we also stop thinking of the word "in" as meaning "inside", or "being contained by", and consider it more in the sense of being "part of" (as for example the colour yellow being "in" a shade of orange; or where two streams have joined, the water of one stream is "in" the water of the other and vice versa), the idea that, through the agency of the Holy Spirit, Christ can be in us and we can be in Him at the same time becomes at least a bit more accessible to our poor brains even if nowhere near fully comprehensible. That understanding is reserved for us in Heaven, when we will see Him as He is. But what is given to us to grasp here and now is that Jesus gave His life to establish a dynamic relationship between Himself and the Church of which He is the Head. This dynamic is mediated by the person of the Holy Spirit, whose sole purpose is to establish the Kingdom of God on Earth on behalf of Jesus, where Jesus and the Father are glorified, and where Jesus, the Father and the Church will all be One. With these thoughts in mind, and not forgetting that picture of the God who is in us that Paul paints at the beginning of the epistle, let us consider some verses from Paul's letter to the Colossians.

"I stand at the door and knock"

When Paul wrote to the Colossians, he also insisted (Col. 4:13) that this message was delivered to the church at Laodicea. There is no knowing how His teaching was received in Colossae, because the city was destroyed in an earthquake in AD 61, three or four years after the epistle was most likely written. But we do know that the church at Laodicea, which Paul felt needed the same teaching, was the "lukewarm" one Jesus speaks to in Revelation 3:14-22. To them He says (probably around five to seven years later, according to most chronologies): "I counsel you to buy from Me gold refined in the fire, that you may be rich; and white garments, that you may be clothed, *that* the shame of your nakedness may not be revealed; and anoint your eyes with eye salve, that you may see" (v.18). This was a church that had been ensnared by the golden ephod instead of seeking the true gold of Christ. This was the church where Jesus said He was standing at the door and knocking. Since none of us want the Lord to vomit us out of His mouth (see Rev. 3:16) it is instructive for us to consider the teaching that they had been given: we need to pay more attention to it than they did, and ask ourselves where it is relevant to the culture of the Church today.

Some parts of the letter refer to issues of morality and carnal behaviour. These are obviously as relevant now as they ever were, but I don't think they have much bearing on the issue of the golden ephod. Other things, such as worship of angels (Col. 2:18), were specific to that cultural context. But if we read verses 16-23 and replace the "regulations" that Paul refers to with some that are current in our Christian life today, we can hear the voice of the Holy Spirit saying to us, with passion: "Hold fast to the Head! Let me build you up in the Spirit! Don't go the way of the Laodiceans!" The verse "Behold, I stand at the door and knock" (Rev. 3:20), so famously depicted in the Holman Hunt painting, has been used by the devil to mislead millions of believers into thinking it's about evangelism, and in doing so he has divested it of its power. It isn't to do with evangelism. The door isn't the door of an unbeliever's heart; it's the door of the lukewarm church.

So often our meetings in the West are not led by the Holy Spirit: they are led by the clock. To the Lord, a day is as a thousand years: there are no clocks in Heaven. I was in Bolivia in 1987, a young Christian, and there was revival going on. I was invited to speak in one of the churches local to where I was staying. Having diligently prepared the message I felt the Lord had given me, imagine how I felt when one of the church leaders got up to speak. I thought he must just be bringing a short prophetic message (I don't speak Spanish), but he carried on for five minutes, ten, fifteen, twenty . . . I realised that this was a full-blown sermon. I had to take a lot of thoughts captive to the obedience of Christ during that time. Eventually he finished. What happened next? Brother Bob from the UK was invited onto the platform, along with a translator. Brother Bob preached the second sermon of that meeting – and the congregation hung on every word. This was not a meeting regulated by the clock: this was a meeting in a country where revival was breaking out. How often would this happen in Europe or the USA? How often have you been in a church meeting and just started to sense the presence of the Lord in the worship when the programme has moved on because it's time for the sermon? Regulations. Jesus, by His Spirit, has stood at the door and knocked – but we haven't let Him in. The lukewarm church, *c'est moi*.

Bread and wine

As I write this it is drawing towards the end the year, and Christmas time. John Betjeman was one of the best-known poets of the 20th century, and a practising Anglican. He concludes his poem "Christmas" with the following lines:

> And is it true,
> This most tremendous tale of all,
> Seen in a stained-glass window's hue,
> A Baby in an ox's stall?
> The Maker of the stars and sea
> Become a Child on earth for me?. . .
>
> For if it is,
>
> No love that in a family dwells,
> No carolling in frosty air,
> Nor all the steeple-shaking bells
> Can with this single Truth compare –
> That God was man in Palestine
> And lives today in Bread and Wine.

Here, in the justly famous lines of a pious churchgoer who wants to believe and wants to follow but just isn't quite sure ("Is it true . . .?"), we probably find the dull reflected gleam of one of the biggest golden ephods of them all: the idea, stronger in some churches than others, that the pinnacle of our experience of the presence of God is in partaking in the sacrament of Holy

Communion. Jesus gave us the bread and the wine as a focal point to gather round as we meet with Him. As we partake of the communion meal we focus on the glory of the cross and the great love freely poured out for us there. Each time we come to the communion table we are edified, we are washed, and we are renewed in our faith and love. This surely is how Jesus meant it to be, when He instructed us to remember Him each time we partake of it. In his final prayer, Jesus said to the Father, "I want those you have given me to be with me where I am, and to see my glory" (John 17:24 NIV). I don't believe that Jesus was talking about His followers seeing Him in Heaven: in the Spirit, we are already where He is. He wants us to live out of that heavenly place of relationship with Him, so we can see His glory on Earth and His Kingdom can be established.

God is so much, so MUCH bigger than any doctrinal box we would like to put Him in. I met with Jesus powerfully, as a non-believer, in a Catholic mass. Anne saw Jesus piercing her heart from across a football stadium, through the eyes of Pope John Paul II. When I was a young Christian, full of the Holy Spirit and prejudice, convinced that anyone who didn't speak in tongues was definitely of no use to the Lord and probably not even saved, He led us sovereignly to spend some time in a large Anglican church where we were loved by many people who had never moved in any gifts of the Holy Spirit. Right at the start of my walk with Him He was dealing with my arrogance towards other brothers and sisters. Although I believe – what this book is all about – that there is a higher level of operation in the Spirit that

Jesus wants to lift us up to for the unfolding of his Kingdom purposes in the last days, I have completely missed it if I ever think I can exalt my spirituality above that of another believer. I'm not even on the ladder, never mind on one of the "higher" rungs.

So we (and I'm addressing myself here) must not, in the pride of our hearts, dismiss traditions just because we do not embrace them ourselves. Nevertheless, when millions of would-be disciples across the world have no higher expectation of an encounter with God than a few minutes every week remembering the cross in a communion service, the enemy has got them exactly where he wants: away from the battle, gathered round a golden ephod, wondering, in their heart of hearts, whether God really exists at all.

The Spirit of Religion

Although we see religion operating among the Pharisees and scribes throughout the gospel accounts, there is probably no clearer cameo of the spirit of religion at work than in John's account of the trial of Jesus, where we read (John 18:28): "Then they led Jesus from Caiaphas to the Praetorium and it was early morning. But they themselves did not go into the Praetorium, lest they should be defiled, but that they might eat the Passover." We may need to read this verse a few times to absorb the shocking truth that it conveys: religion said that the very hands that were delivering the living Paschal Lamb to His death could be kept clean by ritual observance in order to participate in the ceremony that heralded the very event in which they were engaged. This is the great evil of religion: as well as being harsh and unyielding, as well as substituting grace with guilt and freedom with fear, it blinds us to the present reality of the Living God by attempting to satisfy us with the rituals and habits that merely point to Him.

Paul warns the Colossians and Laodiceans not to be deceived by "regulations . . . commandments and doctrines of men . . . tradition of men . . . the basic principles of the world . . . self-imposed religion". He tells us that all of these things are "a deceit" that cheat us of our reward – the reward of the "growth that comes from God" as we "hold fast to the Head" and grow up into Him through the living connections supplied by "every joint and ligament". These living connections that we have with one another and with Him through the Holy Spirit are the opposite of human religion. This passage in Colossians 2 has strong echoes with Ephesians 4, where Paul talks of the five-fold ministries being used by Christ to build His body into perfect unity – into "the perfect man". There are no other passages in all of Paul's letters that resemble each other as closely as these two: they are at the heart of his gospel and his vision of the body of Christ. We have a choice: to grow up into maturity in Christ, or to go the way of the Laodiceans and be spat out of His mouth. We need to allow the Holy Spirit to show us our golden ephods, and throw them out as quickly as we can.

Bible references

Judges 8:27-29
Judges 8:23
Colossians 1:15-21
Colossians 1:26-27
Acts: 17:28
John 17:2-23
John 16:14
Colossians 4:13
Revelation 3:14-22
Revelation 3:16-18
Colossians 2:16-23
Revelation 3:20
John 17:24
John 18:28

PART TWO:
OF THE INCREASE OF HIS GOVERNMENT AND PEACE

From winepress to threshing floor

For every warrior's sandal from the noisy battle,
And garments rolled in blood,
Will be used for burning *and* fuel of fire

For unto us a Child is born,
Unto us a Son is given;
And the government will be upon His shoulder.
And His name will be called
Wonderful, Counsellor, Mighty God,
Everlasting Father, Prince of Peace.

Of the increase of His government and peace
There will be no end,
Upon the throne of David and over His kingdom,
To order it and establish it with judgment and justice
From that time forward, even forever.
The zeal of the LORD of hosts will perform this.

Isaiah 9:5-7

Chapter Twenty-one
The Judgement Seat

Gideon was hiding in the winepress out of fear. When Pilate sat on the judgement seat and handed Jesus over to the Jews to be crucified, he too was in the sway of fear. We are often in the shadow of fear when we sit in judgement over others, which the Bible makes clear is against the will of God at any level. We must allow perfect love to cast out fear, and instead judge our own hearts, to make sure we are in line with the standards of the Holy Spirit, not our own carnal thinking.

When the Midianites are conquered, Isaiah tells us that we will "rejoice before [the Lord] as with joy at the harvest" (Isa. 9:3 esv). The wheat will be on the threshing floor, and not in the winepress. In that place, the Temple of the Lord will stand and we, the Church, will rejoice as one as the manifest presence of Jesus comes among us. Although we all have our personal "Midianites", a look at the account of the crucifixion points clearly to the key players on the enemy team. Jesus was sent to the cross by the Jews and by Pilate. The Jews brought Him to Pilate, and Pilate, albeit reluctantly, handed Him back. Though Pilate famously washed his hands of guilt, the enemy needed to operate through them both to bring about what he thought was the destruction of Jesus. The spiritual powers of destruction that worked against Jesus at His trial are the same that are gathered against the Church today. Although I'm sure that a whole demonic legion was there, baying for the blood of their enemy, there are two powers that we can clearly identify: they are religion, driving the Jews; and fear, driving Pilate.

We have already looked at the idol of religion and seen how it was a snare to Gideon, rendered lukewarm the church at Laodicea, and stalks the Church today. So now we come right back to the winepress where Gideon was hiding, and ask the question again: what about fear?

Pilate found no fault with Jesus and wanted to release Him; but he caved in to the Jews when they said that he was no friend of Caesar if he supported the one who called himself the King of the Jews. "From then on Pilate sought to release Him, but the Jews cried out, saying, 'If you let this Man go, you are not Caesar's friend' . . . When Pilate therefore heard that saying he brought Jesus out and sat down in the judgement seat in a place that is called *The* Pavement, but in Hebrew, Gabbatha" (John 19:12-13). Even while he was on the judgement seat his wife sent him a message that she had received a dream that Jesus was innocent (Matt. 27:19), but any moral integrity he may have had was overwhelmed by the fear that he may lose his career, or even his life; and this fear was powerful enough to cause him to ignore a clear omen that he was making a terrible decision.

Pilate's actions show how strong the connection is between fear and judgement. How often do we sit on the judgement seat over others because ultimately we fear that in some way they will upset the status quo in our own lives? I wonder if the extent to which we judge others is the extent to which we are controlled by fear ourselves? The apostle John writes: "There is no fear in love; but perfect love casts out fear, because fear involves torment. But he who fears has not been made perfect in love" (1 John 4:18). The Greek word *kolasis*, translated as "torment" in the NKJV, has a meaning of correction, punishment, or penalty. In the parable of the unforgiving servant (Matt. 18:23-35), the master gave that servant over to the "tormentors" because he would not forgive his fellow worker. John is telling us that behind every fear is a fear of punishment; and ultimately, one can infer, eternal punishment. This also suggests the converse: that if the love of Christ totally consumes us we will face every situation fearlessly and even willingly go to our deaths for the Lord, which is in fact just what Revelation 12:11 tells us: "And they overcame him by the blood of the Lamb and by the word of their testimony, and they did not love their lives to the death", and what the testimony of all martyrs, from Stephen to contemporary saints, confirms.

Not many of us in these times face losing our lives for our faith in the physical sense, but we are all called to lay down our lives on a daily basis. It is only when we do, that God's *agape* love can flow through us. If there is a scale of sacrificial living from 1-10, where 10 is willingly "not loving our lives unto death", I wonder where I am? Where you are? "I'll give it a 3 today, Lord – maybe a 4 if you're lucky . . . but doing THAT? No, I don't think I'm up for it today, Lord. Sorry!" If our default cross-carrying setting is on 2 or 3, then 5 or 6 will be very hard; 8-9 practically impossible, and 10 – if we have to face it – just won't happen. But if we can truly live at 8-9, then anything less will be easy, and we will embrace 10 if we have to. To live at this level of commitment to Christ, however, we need to be "made perfect in love". If we are fearful, not only are we not made perfect in love, but to a greater or lesser degree we are also (according to 1 John 4:18) living in fear of punishment, and if in fear of punishment, then also in fear of judgement. Out of the fullness of the heart the mouth speaks, as the Lord tells us. A heart full of grace will speak grace. A heart full of fear will speak fear. And a heart under judgement will speak judgement. So fear sits on the judgement seat, and along with religion opposes the fullness of Christ.

Who do you know who sits on the judgement seat? Do you sometimes? I know I do. The passion of Jesus Christ is for His body to be one in heart, so that by our love the world will know that we are His disciples and because of our obedience He and the Father will come and make their home in us (John 14:23). He wants us filled with His Spirit so that we can go out and do the works that He did (and greater – John 14:12), to demonstrate His authority on Earth and assert to the principalities and powers that Jesus Christ is Lord. How can we do this if we judge our brothers? If we judge, we cannot be made perfect in love, fear will be stalking somewhere, and we will be right back there in the winepress.

Yet an internet search for any topic that is in some way related to the fullness of Christ by the power of the Holy Spirit will yield on the first page the writings of those who call themselves teachers, demonstrating by their judgemental words against brothers and sisters in Christ that they have clearly not been perfected in love themselves. Jesus is so clear on this: "Take the log out of your eye," He says, "before you try and take the speck out of your brother's!" (see Matt. 7:5). "Judge not, and then you won't be judged!" We read in Matthew 23:37 how Jesus laments over His beloved Jerusalem because she "kills the prophets and stones those who are sent to her", yet daggers are still out and stones are still flying today, and they will continue to do so all the time religion and fear are free to condemn the life of Christ in the Church. "There is one Lawgiver," says James, "who is able to save and to destroy. Who are you to judge another?" (Jas. 4:12).

We read in 1 Peter 4:17 that judgement begins at the House of God. James warns that we should be circumspect about being a teacher, because those who teach will receive a stricter judgement. The writer to the Hebrews makes it clear that God will chastise us (Heb. 12:6) because His discipline in our lives is an expression of His love as a Father towards His children, and of His passionate desire for us to be made perfect in love. He loves us too much not to bring us face to face with our issues so that He can deal with them and set us free. Both Jesus and Paul give clear guidelines for dealing with sin in the Church, with the ultimate sanction being to remove the persistent sinner from the fellowship of believers. But the purpose in this action is not to judge the sinner by inflicting a penalty on them, but to protect the rest of the body from Satan's influence through their sin. Paul handed Hymenaeus and Alexander over to Satan (1 Tim. 1:20 – we can only guess today what he meant, and many do, but it doesn't sound very pleasant), but it was so that they would "learn not to blaspheme", not so that they would feel the lash of his judgement. Peter saw first-hand how judgement begins at the House of God, when Ananias and Sapphira were so dramatically punished for their deception (Acts 5:1-10); so the words in his first epistle carry the weight of personal experience as well as the anointing of the Holy Spirit. But it is God who judges, not man.

You have read this far, so it is clear by now where I stand theologically in most issues that concern New Testament Christianity. If it isn't I have made a pretty poor job of expressing myself. But the conviction with which I hold to these beliefs is of no value at all if I do not love, genuinely and fervently, those who do not agree with me, because God's band of end-time Gideons will be those who are made perfect in love, not those who are made perfect in the principles of this or any other book written by man. My hope and prayer is that these pages will be helpful to some for whom these principles are acceptable. His loving demonstration of creative miracle power with the communion hosts that I referred to in the last chapter showed me how far above my Protestant charismatic theology are His ways and His thoughts. However great my faith, however accurate my prophecies, however gifted my ministry, however angelic my words: without love, I am nothing.

In the late fourteenth century, the seer Julian of Norwich wrote this:

> "The soul that would preserve its peace, when another's sin is brought to mind, must fly from it as from the pains of hell, looking to God for help against it. To consider the sins of other people will produce a thick film over the eyes of our soul, and prevent us for the time being from seeing the 'fair beauty of the Lord' – unless, that is, we look at them contrite along with the sinner, being sorry with and for him, and yearning over him for God. Without this it can only harm, disturb, and hinder the soul who considers them."

(*Revelations of Divine Love,* available in Penguin Classics)

If I sit in the judgement seat over your relationship with God, there is something in my life that doesn't belong. There is wheat in the winepress, and perfect love has to cast it out.

By what standard?

Thinking Fast and Slow is a book by the Nobel Prize winner Daniel Kahnemann. Drawing on a wide range of psychological research by himself and others he demonstrates conclusively that the brain has two distinct systems for processing information. System one is the complex array of automatic, intuitive, subconscious programmes by which we make sense of the world and look for coherence on a minute-by-minute basis; system two is the reflective, analytical faculty by which we consciously process data, check system-one models for inconsistencies, and operate functions like self-control. For most people, system one knows that 2+2=4; and – again for most people – system two is needed to work out the answer to 17 x 23. System two tends to be lazy, and will rubber-stamp system-one decisions much of the time if they appear plausible. Using a flying analogy, system one is autopilot which any airliner runs on most of the time; system two is the pilot's control of more complex manoeuvres such as landing and take-off.

One morning Anne and I were away on a business trip and were ordering breakfast in a hotel. The waiter and I got our wires crossed, and he came back with the wrong order. When I was explaining the problem I felt the need to be quite assertive to gain his full attention. When he went away to put the matter right I felt quite pleased with my efforts. I had taken control and put things straight: it was, of course, all the waiter's fault. However, the look on Anne's face suggested that she did not share my feelings. "What's the matter?" I said. "It's all sorted now. I got everything right, didn't I?"

Before Anne could answer, the Lord spoke three words into my heart. "By what standard?" He said. Yes, I had sorted out our breakfast order and got everything I wanted. But in doing so I had clearly judged the waiter as incompetent and displayed that in my attitude to him. God's thoughts and His ways are so much higher than ours. Love is His standard. While we are busy judging others on how well they are treating us, He is judging us on how much we are loving them. Paul exhorts us (Rom. 12:2) not to be conformed to the patterns of the world, but to be transformed daily by the renewing of our minds. In the wonderful doxology of Philippians 2, he tells us that we must have the mind in us "which was also in Christ Jesus". In over thirty-five years of being a Christian, I have consistently struggled with these verses – and Anne has struggled with the (lack of) results. No matter how much I wanted my brain to go down different tracks, especially to reflect on my thoughts before I spoke them out, my habits of communication on a personal level just did not seem to be an expression of a renewed mind, the mind of Christ.

In the amazing complexity of His creation, however, God has even provided for this. We do not have to use a thinking system that is "conformed to the world" to pick itself up by its bootstraps and suddenly become conformed to the pattern of Heaven. For some people, of course, salvation works this in them immediately, because God can and will do whatever He chooses; but for those of you for whom, like me, this has been an area of ongoing struggle, here is the good news: your system one may be stuck in the ways of the world, but you also have a system two which can take those three words that God gave me and say to those self-centred programmes which still seem to run your life: "By what standard am I operating?" God's thoughts and God's ways – the thought-processes of the mind of Christ – do not always come to us automatically. System two is naturally lazy, and the devil likes to keep it like that. But God has given it to us so that we can look at ourselves and consciously conform to His standards instead of living under, and subjecting others to, our own. We don't need to read the book (although I recommend it) to understand the principle; God has created us with the capacity for reflection, and He asks us to use it. If we can keep activating system two we can sit on the judgement seat over ourselves and really live by 2 Corinthians 10:5, taking every thought captive to the obedience of Christ so that we can guard against fear and judgement spoiling our harvest.

Bible references

Isaiah 9:3

John 19:12-13

Matthew 27:19

1 John 4:18

Matthew 18:23-35

Revelation 12:11

John 14:23

John 14:12

Matthew 7:5

Matthew 23:37

James 4:12

1 Peter 4:17

Hebrews 12:6

1 Timothy 1:20

Acts 5:1-10

Romans 12:2

Philippians 2:5

2 Corinthians 10:5

Chapter Twenty-two
The Zeal of the Lord

It is only the flame of God's zealous love burning within us that can make us "violent" enough to take on the mantle of Gideon and seize the Kingdom back from the enemy who stole dominion in the Garden of Eden. This is the nature of the divine love that is poured out into our hearts by the Holy Spirit and gives us the intensity by which we can be salt and light.

The fame of Gideon's victory extends beyond the record of the book of Judges. Isaiah comes back to "The Day of Midian" in chapter 10 verse 26: "And the LORD of hosts will stir up a scourge for him like the slaughter of Midian at the rock of Oreb", and in Psalm 83, where the psalmist prays: "Make their nobles like Oreb and like Zeeb, yes, all their princes like Zebah and Zalmunna, who said, 'Let us take for ourselves the pastures of God for a possession. O my God, make them like the whirling dust, like the chaff before the wind!'" (Ps. 83:11-13). Many prophetic voices today would say that God is preparing the Church for history's final confrontation between darkness and light, and is raising up the Gideons of this generation who will carry the banner for Jesus and see the works of the evil one destroyed in His name. But the aim of defeating the enemy is not just that we can reclaim our "pastures" and live in prosperity, health and happiness: it is that Jesus should be glorified. The psalmist continues: "That they may know that You, whose name alone is the LORD, are the Most High over all the earth" (Ps. 83:18). Every stronghold pulled down is ground gained for the King. Wherever the light has overcome the darkness it brings glory to the Lord. The glorious cause we are fighting for is the increase of the Kingdom of God. It's time to leave the shelter of the winepress behind and feel the wind on the threshing floor.

Read Isaiah 9:6-7 again. Ultimately, what is it that increases the government of Jesus? What is it that builds the Kingdom of God on Earth? The victories that we win in the name of Jesus take the ground and glorify His name, but there is another, higher element above them all; an over-arching rallying cry from Heaven that is the primary thrust of the increase of the Kingdom of God, and without which no Gideon will prevail. The only thing that will "perform this" is "the zeal of the Lord of Hosts". The perfect love that drives out fear and the zeal of the Lord are one and the same passion.

The primary meaning of the word "zeal" used here refers to sexual passion or ardour. Our God is a jealous God: He refers to Himself in the Old Testament as Israel's husband, betrayed by her unfaithfulness (as illustrated for example in the book of Hosea); and Jesus is the coming bridegroom whose marriage is the culmination of the entire Bible story. In *Zechariah 1:14 the Lord of Hosts says,* "I am zealous for Jerusalem and for Zion with great zeal." All the passion in the word of God points forward to the marriage of the Lamb to His prepared, perfected bride. How does the bridegroom say His Kingdom will increase while the bride is being prepared?

He tells us the gates of Hell will not prevail against it: His warrior army will bring Him glory. "Thanks be to God, who *always leads us* in His *triumph* in Christ, and manifests through *us* the sweet aroma of the knowledge of Him in every place" (2 Cor. 2:14 NASB). But while Isaiah proclaims that it is only "the zeal of the Lord that will accomplish this", the zealous Lord Himself tells us (Matt. 11:12) that "the Kingdom of heaven suffers violence, and the violent take it by force". When Jesus made this well-known statement he had just commanded the twelve to go out and preach the kingdom of God: "And as you go, preach, saying, 'The kingdom of heaven is at hand.' Heal the sick, cleanse the lepers, raise the dead, cast out demons. Freely you have received, freely give" (Matt. 10:7-8). What they had just "freely received" was His authority to demonstrate the life-giving power of this Kingdom (Matt. 10:1). When, a short while later, John's disciples came to ask Jesus whether He really was the coming Messiah who would usher in the kingdom of God, He pointed to the works that were being done – the sick healed, demons cast out, the dead raised – as proof of His credentials. In His reference to the Kingdom of heaven "suffering violence" and being "taken by force" by "the violent", His time-frame was very specific: He said that this had been happening since the days of John the Baptist until the time He was speaking. The word used here, *Harpazō, means to* seize on, or eagerly lay claim to. There appears to be an inescapable logic here: those violent ones, whose way was prepared by John the Baptist, were Jesus and His disciples. No other human being in the world at that time had the power and authority to bring the light of Heaven to the darkness of Earth. Jesus possessed it because the Father had given it to Him (John 3:35), and He in turn freely gave it to His disciples. The scope of that Kingdom authority was extended when He sent out the 70 a little later; again on the mount of ascension when He commissioned His followers to go into all the world; and finally when He delivered it to the Church through the Holy Spirit. We are sent out with the authority to claim back what is ours in Christ.

Consuming fire

However, Jesus's words in Matthew 11:12 imply that this authority and power (the Greek word *exousia* combines both meanings) that we have been given to extend the Kingdom of God has to be used in a particular way: that is, with "violence". The Greek word used means ardent zeal, intense exertion, or earnest effort. Isaiah 9:7 tells us that it is the "zeal of the LORD" that will perform the increase of God's Kingdom. This increase of the kingdom of Heaven on Earth began when Jesus sent out the 12: before then it resided in Jesus alone. Jesus is jealous for His bride! As the one who knows the beginning from the end He surely looks down through history and sees her in her radiant perfection when the marriage of the Lamb is fulfilled. What burning jealousy, what ardent zeal He must feel to see her still covered with the filth and scars of Satan's stolen dominion in this present age! No wonder He said (Luke 12:49), "I came to send fire on the earth, and how I wish it were already kindled!"

So it is only with the zeal of the Lord of Hosts that we can wield the authority of the name of Jesus, so that the dominion of the evil one can be broken, the Kingdom of Heaven extended on earth, and His bride released, restored and perfected. When the seventh angel sounded the trumpet (Rev. 11:15) John heard loud voices in Heaven proclaiming: "The kingdoms of this world have become *the kingdoms* of our Lord and of His Christ, and He shall reign forever and ever!" Satan taunted Jesus in the wilderness by reminding Him (Luke 4:6) that all the authority and glory of the kingdoms of the world had been delivered to him (referring to the temptation and fall of man). Taking the Kingdom "by force" doesn't mean we take it from God; it means we wrestle it back from the devil. We have to lay hold of what is rightfully ours and force the enemy to let go. Satan is not going to roll over as soon as we come onto the scene, particularly if he has been enjoying a particular stronghold for a long time: it is only the zeal of the Lord of Hosts that will "perform this". The enemy needs to know we mean business. He is a legalist. Unless we really do have the passion of Jesus for the increase of His kingdom burning like a fire in our hearts he will just say, "You don't really mean business: I'm not going anywhere," and unfortunately he will be right. He knows the Scriptures better than we do. He knows that only the zeal of the Lord can take back what he stole.

Although we can relate the meaning of zeal to the human experience of jealous love, we cannot begin to pretend that we have the capacity in our human hearts for the zeal – the ardour – of the Lord. But God has thought of this, and so it isn't a problem, because "the love of God has been poured out in our hearts by the Holy Spirit who was given to us" (Rom. 5:5). We often, rightfully, quote this well-known scripture to remind ourselves that the *agape* love that Christ demonstrated on the cross comes to us from God by the Holy Spirit. But we tend to focus on the compassion of Jesus, and not the passion. Because the character of the Holy Spirit is so gentle and tender, we can forget that our God is also "a consuming fire" (Heb. 12:29). And when we do think about that fire, it tends to be in the context of the fire that burns up sin, or devours the wood, hay and stubble of works that we build in our own strength (see 1 Cor. 3:12). But we need to remember that the Holy Spirit burns with the fire that Jesus longed to see raging on the Earth: it's the fire of His passion for His bride; the jealousy with which He views His stolen property and is urging us forward to lay hold of it and give it back to Him. We need to seek the fire of His passion, and give Him permission to burn in us.

Being salt

It only took 300 men to destroy the hordes of Midian. Like a pinch of salt in a pot of stew, it was enough. We are told (Matt. 5:13) that we are the salt of the earth, and Jesus makes it clear that we must not lose our "saltiness". What I know about salt is that if I put just a little bit in my mouth I will soon be rinsing it out with a glass of water because the flavour is so strong, but if I put it in the stew I'm cooking it will change the flavour from bland to just what the recipe intended, because it will bring all the other ingredients to life. Salt is NOTHING IF NOT INTENSE. Whatever else it might also be, our "saltiness" is our intensity. Jesus says to us, His disciples, that if we lose our intensity what can be added to the world to bring it to life? Nothing. It's not just that we are salt; we are THE salt. We salt the Earth with the zeal of the Lord.

Being salt is not just about evangelism. The passion with which Jesus burns for the world is the same as the love He wants to see released in the Church, so that our love for one another shows the world that we are His disciples. Peter makes this clear in his first letter to the Church: "Since you have purified your souls in obeying the truth through the Spirit in sincere love of the brethren, love one another *fervently* with a pure heart" (1 Pet. 1:22). The Strong's reference for *ektenos,* the Greek word translated as "fervently", is earnestly, fervently, intensely. This is a love that goes beyond coffee after church. If the world is going to see our love for one another, there has to be something deep, something special, about it. A genuine relationship is a private commitment between individuals. This can be between two people, or can extend to a small group. God isn't asking us to parade our church membership before the world – the world has had plenty of that and is not impressed. What He is asking is that the intensity of His love in our hearts for each other so pervades our lives that it is visible to outsiders who come into contact with us. When the disciples "sold their possessions and goods, and divided them among all, as anyone had need" (Acts 2:45) it was accompanied by the Lord "adding daily to the church those who were being saved" (Acts 2:47). The world saw the intensity of the love in the Church. People tasted the salt.

I love scented plants, especially roses. In our garden we have roses, honeysuckle and jasmine, and it's my delight to walk among them and catch the scents on the breeze. We also have dustbins at the side of the house, just inside our gate. On one occasion a packet of chicken had fallen behind the bins into an area that was concealed by an overhang of plants. It must have been there for at least a month – and this was during a (mostly – this is England) warm summer spell – until I discovered it. I did not delight in walking past those bins, and I couldn't understand why the revolting smell that pervaded that area did not go when I took the bins down to the roadside to be emptied. We have an aroma, "the fragrance of Christ" that reaches the Father (2 Cor. 2:15). We read that in the world this is either the fragrance of life or the stench of death, depending on whether or not the people it reaches are on the path leading to life or to death. So we're either scented roses, or rotting meat. If our love is intense, we should not be surprised if "those who are perishing" are sometimes driven away: this is the reaction that scripture leads us to expect. Indeed if they are not, I would say that we need to examine the intensity of the flames that burn within us. I see roses in the supermarket every day, but I neither avoid them nor pick them up: I just walk past. They have no aroma. If we have no intensity, we have no aroma, and people will just walk past us. They see the Church every day; they know what it looks like, but if there is no aroma there is nothing to draw them closer and encourage them to "taste and see" the goodness of God. We see supermarket roses in the book of Revelation: Laodicea, the lukewarm church.

If we need to be reminded of the radical nature of the love that is poured out into our hearts by the Holy Spirit we only need to turn to 1 John 4, where the apostle makes it clear that the love of God that abides in us by the Holy Spirit is the love that took Jesus to the cross to pay for our sins so that "we might live through Him" (v.9). Jesus tells us that He is the vine, and we are the branches – that we can do nothing without Him. On the other hand, with God everything is possible (Luke 18:24-26). If we live through our own efforts, we achieve nothing except exhaustion; if we live through Christ we achieve the impossible: we can achieve the impossible works of faith, to see the lost saved, the sick healed, the bound set free and the dead raised; and we can achieve the impossible works of love, to be led like a lamb to the slaughter when our souls cry "that's not fair!", to give our shirt as well to the scrounger who didn't even deserve the coat, to forgive the ones who wrong us seventy times seven, to offer the olive branch when the wisdom of the world shouts condemn. If we can love in the small impossible things, we can love in the greater ones. The next chapter explores in more detail what it means to live through Christ.

It seems fitting that "the disciple whom Jesus loved" should be entrusted by the Holy Spirit with the extended treatise on the love of God that we find in his first epistle. To read it is like gazing into a river of water where every drop is crystal clear, yet where the depth is such that you cannot see the bottom. It was the first book of the Bible I ever read, before I was a Christian and was deep into New Age teachings. I didn't understand it, but was struck by the power of the truth I sensed it carried, and I wanted more: if you know any New Age adherents, have them read 1 John. Chapter 4 is the "God is love" chapter: John tells us that this great love that God has shown us compels us to love one another; that we cannot claim to love God unless we do, and indeed that we demonstrate our love for God by keeping His commandment to love one another. In an echo of the words of Christ that John records in chapter 14 of his gospel account, he tells us that we abide in God and God in us when we keep this commandment. John returns repeatedly to the phrase "by this we know . . ." Effectively He gives us three markers, like the three legs of a stool, by which we know that this is the truth: one, if we acknowledge that Jesus is the son of God it means that we are born of God (4:15; 5:1); two, we have received His Spirit (4:13); and three, as referenced above, that if we keep His commandment to abide in love for one another it means we also abide in His love and He in us (4:16). All three are essential.

In Isaiah 9:2-7 we see unfolded the narrative of everything that "the zeal of the Lord of Hosts will perform". We see a great light shining in the darkness. We see the Day of Midian established as a template for the Adversary's defeat and we see the joy of harvest and multiplication that ensues from that victory. We see all our pains and sorrows ("every garment rolled in blood") submitted to the Holy Spirit to be used as "fuel of fire". And we see all this because Jesus was sent to Earth to begin the unstoppable mission of the increase of His Kingdom. God is so zealous for us, His love so ardent, that He gave His only Son so that we might live through Him and His love be perfected in us to the extent that our sonship is as true in the world as the sonship of Jesus Christ Himself. What an amazing assertion to take hold of: in this world we are to the Father just as Jesus is (1 John 4:17). John writes (1 John 5:20) that "we know that the Son of God has come and has given us an understanding, that we may know Him who is true; and we are in Him who is true, in His Son Jesus Christ". John is writing about experience, not theory or information. He is telling us that to be "in Christ" is also to know the depth and passion of His love. His point is clear: to know this love in truth is to walk in it ourselves. Human zeal spells division, disaster and death, but to walk in divine zeal is to be one of the "violent" warriors who take the Kingdom back from the enemy.

Bible references

Isaiah 10:26

Psalm 83:11-13

Psalm 83:18

Isaiah 9:6-7

Zechariah 1:14

2 Corinthians 2:14

Matthew 11:12

Matthew 10:7-8

Matthew 10:1

John 3:35

Revelation 11:15

Luke 12:49

Luke 4:6

Romans 5:5

Hebrews 12:29

1 Corinthians 3:12

Matthew 5:13

1 Peter 1:22

Acts 2:45,47

2 Corinthians 2:15

Luke 18:24-26

1 John 4:13 – 5:1, 5:20

Chapter Twenty-three
Living Through Christ

The God-given context for the life of faith is *agape* love. God's *agape* raised up Gideon to bring deliverance to His beloved people, and it's His *agape* that raises up Gideons in the body of Christ today. Where *agape* flows, fruitful works of faith can follow. We are not just commanded to love one another as love is known in the world; we are called to *agape* one another as love is defined in Heaven. Unless we do, we are not living out the faith that we profess.

At the beginning of the Judges account, the people of God are cowering in fear of their enemy; and at the end the enemy has been completely cast out. We know that perfect love casts out fear and that there is no fear in love; and we know that where fear remains love is not perfected and there is still wheat in the winepress.

God is love, so nothing of God can be expressed without love. God's word is the ultimate authority in the universe, and we can have absolute faith in the truth and authority of that word, settled in Heaven – but we also know from Galatians 5:6 that faith must work through love, and that nothing else counts. It is only in the context of following the way of love that we can eagerly desire the spiritual gifts (see 1 Cor. 14:1).

John writes at length about God's love being perfected in us. The story of Gideon shows us how God's perfect love for His people drives out the enemy through one man being transformed by the zeal of the Lord. For God's love to be perfected in us, that must mean that the love that we carry in our hearts by the Holy Spirit is zealous, passionate and burning, like his own. Otherwise it is an imperfect match, supermarket roses, form without power. Jesus is the way, the truth and the life. He is the perfect incarnation of the zeal of the Lord. His way is love: His passionate perfect love is the love that will drive out our Midianites; there is no other. His word is truth. His life is the eternal life of the Holy Spirit who dwells in our hearts. God gave us His son so that we could live through Him. The only way to live through Jesus is in the truth of

His word that we obey and declare, and the zeal of His love, by the power of His Spirit.

We sing about God's unfailing love. We proclaim our love for Him. We pray for healing and deliverance. We believe God for miracles, for signs and wonders confirming His word. We read and declare John 14:13, that our Father will give us whatever we ask in the name of Jesus. And then when it seems that He hasn't, we rationalise it away. We say that our faith is too weak, or that we should have prayed "harder" (whatever that means...), or that God's ways are higher than ours, or that it is all in His hands, or a hundred other reasons as to why God hasn't given us what we have asked, even though He said He would. But how often do we look at the basic issue of the extent to which we are obeying His command to love one another? We claim James 5:16 – the effectiveness of the fervent prayer of a righteous man – but if faith only works through love that fervency must relate to the love that is driving our prayer. If our prayers are not as effective as this verse says they should be, is it the fervency that is missing in our hearts? Are we missing our fragrance? Because it is only the zeal of the Lord that will build His Kingdom.

This is not a moment for us to look at ourselves and to say we are failures. If the fragrance of Christ's zealous love is missing from our lives and we do not recognise the fact, then yes, the analogy of the supermarket rose might apply. But if we do see our lack and yield our hearts to the Holy Spirit's fire we are not supermarket roses at all – we are tight green buds that have yet to come into bloom. Green buds have no scent either. I believe that this, for the most part, is the state of the Church today; that this is how Jesus would see us, and that His Spirit is already at work bringing us into glorious full fragrant bloom. When we step back from individual verses and see how one theme is stamped all over the pages of the New Testament it is clear that Christian life – life in the Spirit, the abundant life that Jesus promises us – is only worked out when we are in a relationship of love with others in the body. Here are a few paraphrased verses which you will probably recognise:

> Jesus is present in the midst of two or more who are gathered together. We know God abides in us when we love one another. We are branches of a single vine whose life flows through us all. God dwells in us and His love is perfected in us when we love one another. Jesus prayed that we would be "perfect" (that perfection word again) in unity, as He and the Father are one. Jesus gave ministries to the Church to build us up in love and unity until we reach the perfection of our full stature in Christ. One part of the body does not tell another part it isn't needed, but each one honours and works with the others.

His commands are not burdensome

And so on. No prizes for finding the Bible references. Jesus commanded us to love each other as He loved us. He didn't say it's an option, He said "that's an order". The scriptures referenced above show us that the whole point of church is to create the context in which this is possible. Just in case there was any doubt,

John reminds us (1 John 3:23) that the Father requires just two things from us: that we believe in His Son, and that we do as Jesus told us, namely to love one another. I think the phrase that we might skip over is "as I have loved you". That means passionately, ardently, with zeal, fervently – choose your adverb. As I have already said, it means more than coffee after church, or going to small group once a week. The thing is, John tells us that His commands are "not burdensome", and they are not burdensome, he says, because we have overcome the world (1 John 5:3) through our faith in Jesus. This means that the only things that can make His commandments burdensome come from the world and the spiritual forces that rule it. So why do we often find it so difficult to follow the kingdom-building promptings of the Spirit of Love? Well, here is an example of where I, for one, missed it.

I was in town with my sister-in-law, her husband and their daughter who at the time was going through some difficulties. They all love the Lord, and are hungry for more of the reality of the presence of God than they are experiencing in their church. We had planned to meet up with Anne at a certain place, but then plans changed and we went back to the car park only a few minutes after parking the car. Everyone was feeling a little frustrated, but I said, light-heartedly but as it turns out prophetically, "Not to worry. God has a purpose for this!" When we got to the car park, our church youth pastor was there with his 12-year-old son rummaging through his pockets, looking for his parking chip coin. The Lord told me he wasn't going to find it, and to pay the £20 he would need to get his car out without it. Two other voices spoke at the same time.

One said, "He's bound to find it!" and the other said, "You can't offer to pay for him – he would be embarrassed!" I listened to those two, ignored the Holy Spirit, made some passing comment and we went on our way. He told me later he never found the chip coin. So instead of witnessing on multiple levels of the Holy Spirit's activity and the Father's loving provision in our everyday lives – encouraging my spiritually thirsty relatives, blessing the youth pastor, being a witness to his son and building my niece in her faith, all for the price of a mere £20 – I came under the influence of the ruler of this world, agreed with his lies, and didn't bear any fruit that would glorify the Father (John 15:8). I even said to my sister-in law, "Look, I said God has a purpose!", and introduced them to Stephen, enjoying the "spiritual" moment, but instead of releasing the fragrance of Christ, I hardened my heart. God's purpose was not in the superficial and meaningless introductions, but in the small act of love that would not have been burdensome but would have had a real effect on the lives of five people.

In giving us victory over the world through our faith in Christ, God has also given us the ability to overcome the siren calls of the world's voices. The Holy Spirit within us always wants to reach out in love. The world always wants that love to be quenched. We need to learn how to ignore its deceiving voice, and believe that God's command to love is not burdensome. If we sense that God has a purpose in a situation where we find ourselves, we need to wait in there until we see it fulfilled somehow in an expression of His love. In my case, it was a gift of £20, not just a few handshakes. Unfortunately, I think we often go all too readily for the handshake, and the gift remains ungiven.

The apostle John makes it clear, both in his gospel account (especially chapters 14 – 15), and in his letters (especially 1 John 4 – 5) that we cannot love Jesus unless we obey His command to love one another. Jesus spells it out in the extended metaphor of the vine: to remain in His love we need to love one another and live by His words – which is what is meant by His words "remaining in us". The same Holy Spirit wrote in Proverbs 22:17-19: "Apply your heart to My knowledge; for it is a pleasant thing to keep them [God's words] within you; let them all be fixed upon your lips, so that your trust may be in the LORD; I have instructed you today, even you." The voices of the world want to pluck God's words from our lips and smother them in our hearts, so that we feel cut off from the love flowing in the vine and our faith is fruitless. To carry out God's promptings to love we need to discern and ignore the voices of the world that we have overcome. We cannot live through Christ unless we live through His love; we cannot live through His love unless we love one another; we cannot love one another without obeying His commands; we cannot obey His commands if we tune them out. As we saw in chapter thirteen, a warrior must be a listener.

Agape

In Jesus's last discourse to His disciples, recorded in John 14 – 16, He tells us repeatedly that we love Him if we keep His commandments; that His commandment is that we love one another; that we will receive from the Father whatever we ask in prayer; that we are to remain in Him and in His love; and that He has chosen us to bear fruit. These great themes are all intertwined in one fabric: pull out one thread and the whole cloth unravels. John 14:21 expresses it well: "He who has my commandments and keeps them, it is he who loves Me. And he who loves Me will be loved by My Father, and I will love him and manifest Myself to him." Isn't this what we long for, the manifestation of Jesus in our midst? As I mentioned earlier in this chapter, He promises that He will be in our midst where two or three of us are gathered in His name (Matt. 18:20). It's important that He talks about two or three being gathered – in other words, where there is relationship. It has often been said that the Bible is about two relationships: Man with God, and Man with Man. I think we can read the beginning of the book of Acts and focus on the works of God rather than His ways, but it's as important to us in these days that the disciples had all things in common (Acts 2:44), or that Barnabas sold a field and gave the proceeds to the Church (Acts 4:37) as it is that Peter and John healed the man at the Gate Beautiful. We need to reclaim the true meaning of fellowship, not as an article of religion, but as a holy desire to give in faith and freedom so that others are blessed, in the sure knowledge that God will give back to us "pressed down . . . and running over" (Luke 6:38), as Jesus has promised.

Agape was not a common word in New Testament times. Other than the usage with which we are familiar it was rarely, if ever used. It is that great love which God had for the world which took

Jesus to the cross, and it is the love that Jesus commanded us to have for one another. The word "love" is common currency in our culture, and is tainted by Hollywood, TV soaps, social media and the rest. It is loaded with human emotion and associations. To even use it in the context of God's passion for us is to risk humanising the Divine, whose ways really are not ours at all. (How many times do we need to remind ourselves of this?) As Christians, let's keep "love" for our pillow talk and greetings cards. What we are called to is *agape*.

It is fitting that John, the "apostle of love", was also nicknamed one of the "sons of thunder" (Mark 3:17). The *agape* that takes the Kingdom back from the enemy who stole it is fierce. It roars like thunder. If we are gathered in the name of the God who is *Agape*, that means the people gathered have to be loving each other in truth, as He commanded – if not, then they are not gathered in His name. In other words, Jesus promises that He will be present among us where *agape* is flowing in the body in the same way that it flowed in the accounts of the book of Acts. This is the life that runs through the Vine: fervent *agape* love that expresses God's heart; zealous love, Barnabas love, thunder love.

The Ichthus symbol has been used by Christians as a badge of identity since the second century. As you probably know, the word Ichthus is an acrostic of the Greek words for Jesus Christ Son of God Saviour, and the actual word, used commonly in the New Testament, means "fish". If we are fish, then *agape* is our water. We need to stay immersed in it.

Bible references

Galatians 5:6

1 Corinthians 14:1

John 14:13

James 5:16

1 John 3:23

1 John 5:3

John 15:8

Proverbs 22:17-19

John 14:21

Matthew 18:20

Acts 2:44

Acts 4:37

Luke 6:38

Mark 3:17

Isaiah 9:6

Chapter Twenty-four
The Torch

Jesus was sent to bring the burning torch of *agape* to Israel; the mission of the Church is to carry the torch into the rest of the world. The Holy Spirit anointed Jesus for His work; He anoints us for ours. He alone is the Torch that lights the fire with which Jesus longed to set the world alight. Since Pentecost it's been the turn of the Church to carry the Torch.

We have followed Gideon "from faith to faith", from his meeting with the Lord while he cowered in the winepress, through his lessons of faith and provision, to the final victory which earned "the Day of Midian" its place in the messianic prophecy of Isaiah 9 as a pattern for breaking the power of the enemy and claiming back the Kingdom for Christ. We have seen also that it is only "the zeal of the Lord" – His ardent, perfect agape – that will enable us to walk in the truth and power of the lessons that Gideon learnt and also break the stranglehold of religion and fear that still throttles the flow of the blood of Christ in much of the life of the Church. We have left the winepress behind and joined the band of warriors at the threshing floor. Now what?

Let's go back to the moment when Gideon, full of faith, proclaimed God's victory: "A sword for the LORD and for Gideon!" As one, the army uncovered their jars, and fire burned all around the enemy camp. Ultimately, it's all about the fire. A fire of love – the very word "ardent" comes from the Latin word for "burning" – burns in the heart of God. Deuteronomy 4:24 tells us that "the LORD your God is a consuming fire, a jealous God". His very name is "Jealous" – "You shall worship no other god, for the LORD, whose name is Jealous, is a jealous God" (Exod. 34:14). The Father's jealous love for His people is directed against everything that would threaten them with corruption. We see both sides of this fire in Zephaniah 3:8-20:

> "'Therefore wait for Me,' says the LORD,
> 'Until the day I rise up for plunder;
> My determination is to gather the nations

To My assembly of kingdoms,
To pour on them My indignation,
All My fierce anger;
All the earth shall be devoured
With the fire of My jealousy . . .'" (v.8)

"In that day it shall be said to Jerusalem:
'Do not fear;
Zion, let not your hands be weak.
The LORD your God in your midst,
The Mighty One, will save;
He will rejoice over you with gladness,
He will quiet you with His love,
He will rejoice over you with singing.'" (vs.16-17)

Like Father, like Son . . .

Unsurprisingly, we see the same fire in the Father and the Son. When Jesus appeared to John on the Isle of Patmos, the apostle describes the Lord's eyes as "flames of fire". We have already read how Jesus declares Himself to be "violent", seizing back "by force" the Kingdom that Satan stole in the Garden of Eden (Matt. 11:12). We see His anger blazing at the scribes and Pharisees who have usurped the seat of Moses (Matt. 23:33 NIV): "You Snakes! Brood of Vipers! How will you escape the condemnation of hell?" And we witness the same fury when He enters the Temple and flings out the hawkers and money-lenders. We see the tenderness when He is moved with compassion for the crowds who seem to Him so lost and broken, "like sheep without a shepherd", and when He weeps over Jerusalem, His beloved city. He tells the disciples how He had come "to send fire on the earth", and how He longed for it to be "already kindled" (Luke 12:49 KJV). He was the one who John the Baptist proclaimed would baptise us "with the Holy Ghost and fire" (Luke 3:16). Jesus burned with the love that was in the heart of His Father – the love for the world that took Him to the cross.

So the Father sent Jesus so that He could set the world on fire. But the mission of Jesus was only to bring the zeal of the Lord to one specific group: "the lost sheep of the house of Israel" (Matt. 15:24). When He sends the 12 out to take His fire, He instructs them:

> "Do not go into the way of the Gentiles, and do not enter a city of the Samaritans. But go rather to the lost sheep of the house of Israel. And as you go, preach, saying, 'The kingdom of heaven is at hand.' Heal the sick, cleanse the lepers, raise the dead, cast out demons. Freely you have received, freely give."
>
> (Matt. 10:5-8)

A little later, He again makes it clear: "I was not sent except to the lost sheep of the house of Israel" (Matt. 15:24).

We read another interesting detail concerning Jesus's mission in Acts 10:38: "God anointed Jesus of Nazareth with the Holy Spirit and with power, who went about doing good and healing all who were oppressed by the devil, for God was with Him." It's easy to forget that Jesus, the Son of Man, did not come fully loaded, as it were. It was only when He was baptised that the Holy Spirit came upon Him. That is when God the Father anointed Him with power. First He was sent, and then He was equipped. This is crucial because Jesus tells us, "As the Father has sent Me, I also send you" (John 20:21). The word translated as "also" means "in like manner". The Father sent Jesus and equipped Him to start the fire in Israel, then Jesus sends us "into all the world" to finish the job. As the Father equipped His Son by anointing Him with the Holy Spirit and power, so Jesus equips His brothers in exactly the same way. The first Jewish believers were equipped at Pentecost; the first Gentile believers were equipped when the Holy Spirit came upon them at the house of Cornelius (Acts 10:44-45); and Jesus has been equipping the Church in the same way ever since, anointing us, as the Father anointed Him, "with the Holy Spirit and power".

When Benny Hinn wrote *Good Morning, Holy Spirit*, published in 1990, he brought a radical idea to the Church. It is an idea that is central to our faith; it courses through the Bible from beginning to end; we proclaim it over monotheistic religions and cults such as Islam, Jehovah's Witnesses and Mormonism, and yet we so often seem to grapple with understanding it ourselves. The idea? The Holy Spirit is a person. God the Father, God the Son, God the Holy Spirit. He, the Paraclete, the Comforter promised by Jesus and the Father, the third expression of the Trinity, is the same God as the Father and the Son. Because He is the same God, He has the same character, and His heart burns with the same love. Jesus baptises us with the Holy Spirit and fire because His fire, which is also the Father's fire, is what the Holy Spirit is carrying. The Holy Spirit comes from the Father but it is Jesus who sends Him and it's Jesus whom He reveals (John 16). When the love of God – *agape* – is poured out into our hearts by the Holy Spirit it is so that His fire, the fire of the Father and the fire of the Son, can be ignited within us.

The *agape* of God is like a burning torch. The Father sent Jesus to the lost sheep of Israel and said, "Light the fire here." Then He sent the torch, and Jesus began "the increase of His government and peace" prophesied in Isaiah 9:7. When His work was completed, Jesus returned to the Father, then He passed the torch to us so that we could do the same works, and greater (John 14:12), to take the fire round the rest of the world. Without the torch, we cannot light the fire.

Night of fire

Jesus instructed His disciples to wait for "the Promise of the Father" which, as Joel prophesied, was to pour out His Spirit on all flesh (Joel 2:28; Acts 2:17). He passed the torch on to them on the day of Pentecost. He passed it on to Blaise Pascal on 23rd November 1654.

Pascal was one of the greatest scholars of the 17th century. He was a mathematician, a scientist, and an inventor. Before he was twenty years old he had invented and was selling his own mechanical calculator, and went on to make breakthroughs in probability, fluids and pressure. He is probably best known today in mathematical circles for Pascal's triangle, a simple and elegant *triangular* array of binomial coefficients. Although he'd had an intellectual conversion to Catholicism a few years beforehand he was now less interested in his faith than he was in science and maths. But at around 10.30 p.m. on 23rd November 1654, as he was probably going to bed in a cold, dark room in Paris, the Holy Spirit fell on him and turned his world upside down. For two hours he was consumed by the fire of God. The words he wrote immediately afterwards were found sewn into the lining of his coat after he died nine years later:

FIRE
God of Abraham, God of Isaac, God of Jacob
not of the philosophers and of the learned.
Certitude. Certitude. Heartfelt. Joy. Peace.
God of Jesus Christ.
God of Jesus Christ.
My God and your God.
Your God will be my God.
Forgetfulness of the world and of everything, except God.
He is only truly found by the ways taught in the Gospel.
Grandeur of the human soul.
Righteous Father, the world has not known you, but I
have known you.
Joy, joy, joy, tears of joy.
I have departed from him:

They have forsaken me, the fount of living water.
My God, will you leave me?
Let me not be separated from him forever.
This is eternal life, that they know you, the one true God,
and the one that you sent, Jesus Christ.
Jesus Christ.
Jesus Christ.
I left him; I fled him, renounced, crucified.
Let me never be separated from him.
He is only truly found by the ways taught in the Gospel:
Renunciation, total and sweet.
Complete submission to Jesus Christ and to my director.
Eternally in joy for one day's effort on the earth.
May I not forget your words. Amen

From the moment of this encounter with the Holy Spirit, Pascal put down his intellectual pursuits and devoted his time entirely to writing one of the greatest works of apologetics of all time, known simply as his *Pensées*, or "Thoughts". At a time in history when René Descartes, a contemporary and fellow countryman of Pascal was introducing into the world a radical principle of rationalist thought ("I think, therefore I am") that would become the foundation of modern philosophy and a primary tool of agnostic doubt, and when Jesuit casuistry was leading the Church of the time into a quasi-humanist mire of politically expedient relativism, Jesus Christ poured the love of God out into Pascal's heart by the Holy Spirit and baptised him with fire. The resulting book was an instant success when it was published after his death, and it has been read by millions ever since, both as a work of theology and a work of literature. I studied it myself as an undergraduate doing a degree in French when I was light years from God, and its warmth touched me even then.

"The violent" took the Kingdom by force from the time of Jesus's baptism until His Galilean ministry ("From the time of John the Baptist until now" – Matt. 11:12), and from the day of Pentecost until today it is "the violent", on fire with the passion of the Holy Spirit, who have continued with the mission and will do so until Christ returns. At strategic moments in the history of the nations Jesus has sent the Holy Spirit, on an individual or a group, to fan the flames. John Wesley said that God set him on fire and then people came out to watch him burn. Like Gideon on the mountain, we can do nothing without the fire.

Bible references

Deuteronomy 4:24

Exodus 34:14

Zephaniah 3:8,16-17

Matthew 11:12

Matthew 23:33

Luke 12:49

Matthew 15:24

Luke 3:16

Matthew 10:5-8

Matthew 15:24

Acts 10:38

John 20:21

Acts 10:44-45

Isaiah 9:7

John 14:12

Joel 2:28

Acts 2:17

Matthew 11:12

Chapter Twenty-five
A Most Vehement Flame

Like water to a fish, *agape* is the element in which we have to dwell if we are to see the life of Christ flowing through us in revival. He desires to see our hunger as we call to Him for more of His presence – a hunger that nothing else will satisfy. When the Church is truly filled with Him, not only will His fire have torched the whole earth, but the gospel will have reached every nation – and the bride will be ready for His return.

A t creation, the Spirit of God moved upon the face of the waters and brought this world into being. When the work of creation was finished, God established His king and queen to rule over it. As we know, they allowed the Kingdom to be stolen and they lost their thrones. Now the second Adam has come and established the foundation for the new creation, and since then the Spirit of God has been moving across the face of the waters again to bring it forth. Throughout the centuries, never slumbering nor sleeping, He has been at work, lighting fires, blowing on embers, fanning flames, sustaining His warriors as they carry the torch in their times and bring the "increase of His government and peace". The following are just three examples from fairly recent church history from which I think we can draw some inspiration, bearing in mind that, just as "the nations *are* as a drop in a bucket, And are counted as the small dust on the scales" (Isa. 40:15), so surely are our denomi nations.

Paul tells us (1 Cor. 13:9) that we only prophesy "in part". I think what is true of prophetic words is also true of prophetic signs. Gideon was the anointed leader of God's army. Today, the Lord is calling His army together again. Nearly 150 years ago another army was created that I believe stands as a prophetic sign to us of the work God is doing today.

The army of compassion

Born in Nottingham in April 1829, William Booth was saved at the age of fifteen in a Methodist meeting and embraced the gospel message fervently. Although at the time he was working as an apprentice in a pawnbroker's, he soon felt a call to ministry and began to read widely and study the word of God. In 1849 he left his employment, which he considered sinful, and travelled to London to seek work as a lay preacher. He later became a Methodist minister, and eventually in 1865 he and his wife, Catherine, founded the Christian Revival Society to minister to the poor and destitute in London. In 1878 Booth changed the name of their ministry to the Salvation Army. The rest, as they say, is history. For many of us, the words "Salvation Army" conjure up images of soup kitchens, charity shops, fund-raising mail and uniformed bands performing Christmas carols in the shopping mall. In the public eye it has become another charitable institution alongside many others, Christian and secular, who bring succour to the needy. But William Booth was a Methodist in the manner of the Wesleys, and it was he who wrote this famous song:

Thou Christ of burning, cleansing flame,
Send the fire,
Thy blood-bought gift today we claim,
Send the fire today!
Look down and see this waiting host,
Give us the promised Holy Ghost;
We need another Pentecost,
Send the fire today!

William Booth prayed for the fire to come, and it sent a tide of God's compassion round the world. Along with it comes a sign to believers of the pre-eminence of His compassion in the battle for souls.

There is an interesting sequence in the story of Jesus healing the two blind men (Matt. 9:27-31). First they call out to Him. Second He asks them what they want. Third they ask for healing. Fourth – this is what caught my attention – He had compassion on them. And fifth He opened their eyes. Here's a thought: was it actually the anointing (Acts 10:38, Luke 4:18, Isa. 61:1) that released the compassion from which the healing flowed? So many miracles are preceded by the words "He had compassion" – the healing of the widow's son, the feeding of the five thousand and many more. Of course I'm not inferring that the Son of God had no compassion in His heart without the anointing of the Holy Spirit, but I do think there is a template for us to look at here: anointing, then compassion, then mighty works. If we let the river of God's compassion flow through our hearts it will carry downstream the gifts that we need to do His work.

A sea of divine love

The Azuza Street revival of 1906–1915 was the greatest outpouring of the Holy Spirit in modern times. The fire of God was visibly seen on many occasions, not just by worshippers but by passers-by who called out the fire department. Notable miracles took place, like complete limbs being restored and blind eyes being opened. Thousands were saved and filled with the Holy Spirit. The Pentecostal Church of today was born, and under its banner ministries such as that of Smith Wigglesworth took the message of baptism in the Holy Spirit round the world, with the word confirmed by healings, deliverance and the raising of the dead. The works that Jesus did were done in His name as the fire fell. But the message preached at Azuza Street was not a word of power or healing, or faith, so much as the perfect love of God. Quoting from contemporary eye-witness accounts, Eddie Hyatt writes:

"Walking in God's love was the primary emphasis at Azuza Street. Frank Barleman, a journalist and participant in the revival, described it as a return to the 'first love of the early Church'. (He wrote:) 'Divine love was wonderfully manifest in the meetings. They would not even allow an unkind word against any of their opposers, or the churches. The message was the love of God. It was a sort of "first love" of the early Church returned. The "baptism" as we received it in the beginning did not allow us to think, speak or hear evil of any man. We knew the moment we had grieved the Spirit by an unkind thought or word. We seemed to live in a sea of pure divine love.'"

(From *Fire On The Earth: Eyewitness Reports From the Azusa Street Revival* by Eddie Hyatt, Charisma House, 2006)

The Azuza Street revival was not a bonfire that God just sovereignly lit one day, outside of any historical context; but it followed on the heels of the Holiness movement and the Third Great Awakening, with the preaching of Charles Finney and Dwight L. Moody respectively being notable for their impact. The Holiness movement taught that Christians could achieve perfect sinlessness through the "second blessing" of the Holy Spirit. Some of us would reject that theology today, but in doing so we must be careful not to ignore it altogether: after all Peter reminds us to be holy, as God is Holy (1 Pet. 1:16). Our call is to die to the flesh and walk in the Spirit. At the same time Paul impresses on us that we are not to grieve Him (Eph. 4:30) with our many and varied expressions of carnality. I know that I for one am intellectually aware that the flesh is at war with the Spirit, yet I also know that I am not sufficiently sensitive to His grief whenever I let the flesh win a battle, and as I write this that is something that I am asking the Lord to change in me. We need the sensitivity to the Holy Spirit's feelings that they felt at Azuza Street. If we want to see the power of the Spirit at work in our meetings, we must remember that His name is Holy.

Catching the fire

The final example is the much more recent outpouring that began in January 1994 at the Toronto Airport Vineyard Church and which became known as the Toronto Blessing. The Vineyard Church became the Toronto Airport Christian Fellowship in 1996, and then in 2010 changed its name formally to Catch the Fire. Sparks from the Toronto blaze were soon landing and starting fires all over the world. I have yet to visit Toronto, but I went to various "catch the fire" meetings in the UK in the mid-1990s and experienced first-hand the move of the Holy Spirit that accompanied members of the Toronto team who had been sent out by their church to take the torch with them to the nations.

Common responses to the presence of the Holy Spirit were a deep sense of unexplained joy and release expressed in uncontrollable laughter; an experience of sudden weakness and inability to stand (being "slain in the Spirit") lasting several minutes, or in some cases much longer, and alongside these a succession of healings, deliverances and impartations from the Holy Spirit. An internet search for "Toronto Blessing" or "Catch the Fire" will throw up a fair selection of negative comments, where the words deception, heresy, hysteria and even demonic crop up – as I'm sure they did during the Welsh revival or when Azuza Street was blazing. And it's true that while great joy and physical weakness in the presence of God can be easily referenced in scripture, some other manifestations, such as animal noises that occurred in the same context, are not something that we find so easily, if at all. Fortunately Jesus told us how we "tell a tree" – and it's by the fruit, not by the shape of the leaves or the pattern on the bark. All of us have the treasure of the Kingdom in jars of clay (2 Cor. 4:7), because that is how God has ordained it. We can choose to look for the treasure or look at the jars. The fact is that the Toronto outpouring is still bearing much fruit, and it is fruit that endures (John 15:16). Not only is Catch the Fire itself now a growing international network of churches, but many leaders and ministries who visited Toronto in the early days were greatly impacted at the time and have gone on to become household names in the 21st-century Church – among them Bill Johnson (Bethel), Nicky Gumbel (Holy Trinity Brompton and the Alpha Course), Heidi Baker (over 7,000 churches planted in Mozambique alone and impact for the gospel worldwide), and many more.

The ministry of Heidi Baker is an outstanding example of just how brightly God's compassion burns in the fire of the Holy

Spirit. When she first went to Toronto she had come directly from Mozambique, where Iris Ministries (now Iris Global, which she leads with her husband Rolland) cared for 320 children. She was exhausted, and very ill with double pneumonia. As soon as she walked in, one of the team ministering spoke out from a word of knowledge that a missionary from Mozambique has just arrived, and that the Lord was healing her "right now". In that moment she was totally healed. While she was there she received a vision:

> "I had a vision of Jesus surrounded by a multitude of children He looked at me with His intense, burning eyes of love and I was completely undone. Jesus told me to feed the children, and I began to cry out loud, 'No, there are too many!' He asked me to look into His eyes, and He said, 'I died that there would always be enough.' Then He reached down and broke a piece of flesh out of His right side. His eyes were so magnificently beautiful, yet His body was bruised and broken. He handed me the piece of His flesh; I took it and stretched my hand out to the first child. It became fresh bread. I gave the bread to the children, and they all ate."

(From *Compelled by Love* by Heidi Baker, Charisma House, 2008)

By 2008 the 320 children had become 7,000; now Iris Global feeds thousands more, not just in Mozambique but around the world, along with healings, deliverance, resurrections from the dead, miraculous multiplication of food, and above all the planting of thousands of new churches: this is the fruit of love that can grow when we catch the fire. And interestingly the number of children cared for at that time was roughly the same as the number of churches planted. For every ragged child loved, God gave a congregation. Fruit borne one hundred fold.

The presence of God was manifested as He led the Israelites out of the desert as a pillar of fire. That fire burns in the eyes of Jesus, burns in the flame of the Holy Spirit as He leads us out of the desert today and into the Kingdom of *Agape*. He burns not just for the physically starving in developing countries, but for the spiritually starving in the rich and bloated West. How many of us think we have so much, when like the church at Laodicea we are "poor, naked, and blind"? He longs with such passion for us to turn away from the crumbs that satisfy us and hunger for the banquet He has provided. At communion, we delicately remove a little pinch of bread from the loaf that is passed round. I'm sure what the Lord would love is for us all to pull off great chunks, so that He could multiply the bread as it went round. As He said to Heidi Baker – He died that "there would always be enough".

Our element

The zeal of the Lord of Hosts, the fire of the Holy Spirit which Jesus sends on to the world, and the perfect love, the *agape*, that casts out fear are all bound together: zeal expresses *agape*, *agape* sends zeal. Together they express the passion of the heart of God that yearns for the restoration of His Kingdom and the marriage of the Lamb. This is the love that Jesus tells us to abide in. Like water to fish, as I've already said, the "sea of pure divine love" that they experienced at Azuza Street is actually the element in which we are called to live. It is no coincidence that the greatest miracles happened there when the fire was visibly present.

It is often said that in the developed "free" world we don't see the miracles of healing that seem to be much more the norm in developing countries and the persecuted Church. I, for one – and I think I speak for many here – have always explained this by saying, "We think we don't need faith: we have medicine!" But as we know, Paul tells us that what counts – the only thing that counts – is "faith working through love" (Gal. 5:6). Even if I have the faith that moves mountains, without love I am nothing (1 Cor. 13:2). I don't think it's the faith that sets these churches apart, so much as the love through which it is working. They "love each other fervently, with a pure heart" (1 Pet. 1:22). They need each other, are committed to each other, and are contemporary expressions of the Church of Acts 4. They are one as the Father and the Son are one. Their unity commands the blessing. Because they are obedient to the command to "love one another" they receive what they ask from the Father. They are swimming in that sea of perfect love; they are abiding in Christ, immersed in the river of Ezekiel 47; they are in their element. Am I? Are you? Or are we fish out of water, flapping about on the deck, gasping for life in the Spirit, knowing that there should be more but somehow unable to reach for it?

When John's disciples came to ask Jesus if He really was the Messiah, or if they should "look for another", He told them: *The* blind see and *the* lame walk; *the* lepers are cleansed and *the* deaf hear; *the* dead are raised up and *the* poor have the gospel preached to them." (Matt. 11:5) These things are all happening today, and where they are being seen and heard is where revival fire is burning: we do not "look for another". Three separate prophecies came out of the Azuza Street outpouring pointing to a time 100 years from then, when the presence of God and His glory in the Church would be far greater than anything ever seen. In 1947 Smith Wigglesworth prophesied of the time when the word and the Spirit moving together would bring a revival that, again, would be greater than anything the world has ever seen. In an extended series of visions Rick Joyner saw the final harvest before the return of Christ, when the world economy had completely hit the buffers, law and order had failed worldwide, and at the same time the Holy Spirit was pouring out healing and salvation onto the nations through His powerful presence in an ostracised, multiplying Church. Heidi Baker saw a vision of gold dust being poured out over all the world and people falling on their knees to come to Christ. There is much to suggest that the prophecies from Azuza Street and Smith Wigglesworth (and I'm sure there are many others; these are just two well-known ones that are on my very limited radar) are pointing to the same season, and that we may be moving into it now. If this really is what is happening, there will tragically still be some standing to one side as the fire sweeps across the Earth, clutching their box of matches, saying, "I'm not jumping in there. The flames are the wrong shape!" I do hope I'm not among them. But we have to let *agape* transcend our opinions, our ambitions and even our very desire to see revival: if I don't love the church down the street, even though they may call me a heretic, whatever is going on in my assembly is nothing. If we fail in this any move of God will become religion and we will fall into the trap that caught Gideon.

Wherever it is that we see the fire burning today, or if we look into history and see where it has been, we find the same initial spark: Christians who are hungry for more of God. Not just a little bit more – "If I clear the cluttered desk of my life – actually no, just my church meeting as long as You don't stay too long – a bit, I can fit a bit more of you on this corner, God" – but really MORE; the more that will take us from our dimension into His. "Lord, I'm sweeping everything off my desk. Will You come and fill it? Nothing else will do!"

Søren Kierkegaard, the Danish Christian philosopher and theologian (1813–1855) wrote this:

> "The matter is quite simple. The Bible is very easy to understand. But we Christians are a bunch of scheming swindlers. We pretend to be unable to understand it because we know very well that the minute we understand, we are obliged to act accordingly. Take any words in the New Testament and forget everything except pledging yourself to act accordingly. My God, you will say, if I do that my whole life will be ruined. How would I ever get on in the world?"
>
> (From *Provocations: Spiritual Writings of Kierkegaard*)

The longing of the bride and the groom

The cry of the heart, a two-word prayer, that went out from Toronto and still goes out today was "More, Lord!" Another two-word prayer that I remember singing as a worship song in a UK Catch the Fire meeting in 1995 was "Yes, Lord!". If we want More, first we really need to be hungry: it's "the effective *fervent* prayer of a righteous man [that] avails much" (Jas. 5:16); and second: God wants our total Yes.

The story of Gideon shows us how we can respond when God's fire begins to take hold. If we want to see in the word how the fire starts we need to look elsewhere: not to a New Testament treatise on the Holy Spirit, or to an Old Testament prophecy of Holy outpouring, but to the love poem on the longing of the bride and the groom for one another. As the unfolding of the intimacy between the Shulamite and the Beloved draws to a close, the bride says, in words that encapsulate the essence of the zeal of the Lord:

"Set me as a seal upon your heart,
As a seal upon your arm;
For love *is as* strong as death,
Jealousy *as* cruel as the grave;
Its flames *are* flames of fire,
A most vehement flame."

(Song of Songs 8:6)

The jealous, passionate love of the Father and the Son, burning in the fire of the Holy Spirit – for the bride of the Bible, nothing else will do. Before the Beloved comes to her, He asks for one thing:

"You who dwell in the gardens,
The companions listen for your voice –
Let me hear it!"

(Song of Songs 8:13)

And the bride responds, to end the poem:

"Make haste, my beloved,
And be like a gazelle
Or a young stag
On the mountains of spices."

(Song of Songs 8:14)

Not even Jesus could tell us when He is going to return, but we know two things. One is a collection of signs of the end of the age that He gives us in Matthew 24 – signs which many would say are being fulfilled in our day. The other thing that we know is that He will come in response to hearing our voice. "Let me hear you call me!" says Jesus, the Beloved. "Let me hear you say the words, 'Make Haste, my Beloved!' I want you to be hungry for Me!" At the very end of the Bible we hear the echo of the Shulamite's response: "And the Spirit and the bride say, 'Come!'" And we hear the Beloved say: "Let him who hears say, 'Come!' And let him who thirsts come. Whoever desires, let him take the water of life freely" (Rev. 22:17). It's not just the bride who calls out; it's the Spirit and the bride. Just as Jesus completed the work that the Father gave Him to do at the cross, the Holy Spirit will one day complete the work that He has been given to do on the Earth: the preparation of the bride for the marriage of the Lamb, and the handing over of the kingdoms of the world to the kingdom of our God and His Christ. And as individuals and churches, we are ready when we hear Him ask us to call out to Him. We are ready when we acknowledge that we are thirsty. We are ready when we desire to freely take the water of life. According to the Song of Songs, this will be when we say, "More, Lord; Yes, Lord, nothing but the most vehement flame will satisfy!"

One final thing we can be sure of is this: when holy fire does bring revival to our street, it won't be anything like what we expect. However, in the parable of the ten virgins (Matt. 25: 1-13) Jesus does make it clear what we have to do: we need to be ready for Him with our lamps trimmed and full of oil. This isn't just about trimming wicks: it's about the whole lamp. The Strong's definition of the Greek word for "trimmed", *kosmeō* (from which comes our word "cosmetic"), means to arrange, decorate, adorn, or put in order. In the book of Revelation the seven lampstands represent the seven churches that the risen Lord is walking among (Rev. 1:20). Jesus wants our churches to be brimming with the oil of the Holy Spirit, and beautified with all the fruit of lives laid down, hungry for Him.

The last words of Christ's prayer in the Garden of Gethsemane were this: "I have declared to them Your name, and will declare it, that the love with which you loved Me may be in them, and I in them" (John 17:26). The Greek word *onoma*, "name", means more than just the epithet by which a person is called – it refers to everything associated with the name, including character, rank, and all attributes. Jesus is saying that He has revealed the fullness of the Father to His disciples: as He said, "If you've seen me, you've seen the Father." And He says He will reveal the fullness of the Father in the future: "I will declare it." How? By the Holy Spirit, whom He will send to bring the same revelation that the twelve had when they were with Him. Why? So that His *agape* may be in us. The *agape* of God being poured out into our hearts by the Holy Spirit who is given to us is the fulfilment of John 17:26. Jesus tells us that it is by our love that the world will know we are His disciples. I don't think that this is about the world looking at us and just seeing how much we love each other, or even looking at our humanitarian efforts and seeing how much we love the world. It means that when we truly walk in His *agape* WE WILL DO THE WORKS THAT HE DID, and revival will follow. This was Heidi Baker's experience in Mozambique, and surely this is true discipleship.

Paul prayed (Eph. 3:14-21) that we would be filled with all of God – the "fullness" of God, meaning that no aspect of the Divine nature (see 2 Pet. 3-4) would be missing from our lives. This fullness comes from yielding our vain understanding to the truth that the *Agape* of Christ goes beyond anything we can humanly grasp; that it surpasses or goes beyond anything that we can call knowledge. Paul begins by praying that, with all the riches of His glory at His disposal, God would give us the supernatural ability, the *dynamis* power, to enable the faith to rise in our hearts that Christ will make His home there as He promises (John 14:23). Paul uses the word *katoikeō,* meaning to dwell, inhabit, be always present. This prayer, for them and for us, is that the indwelling Christ would become a present, manifest reality in our lives so that *agape* can become the foundation for all we are and all we do; that Jesus would hold our gaze with that most vehement flame, reaching out through us with supernatural gifts to the people we are with, lifting our hearts into heavenly glory as we worship, and opening the storehouses of Heaven to all our needs as we bring His fire to the Earth.

We are rooted and grounded in *agape* when the manifest presence of God is a reality in our lives and we walk in intimacy with Him, and this can only happen when we fully die to ourselves and yield our hearts to the mighty power of the Holy Spirit. Without *dynamis* there is no Gideon's army and there is no *agape*; and without *agape* there will always be wheat in the winepress.

A picture has been with me as I have been thinking about this over the last few days, and it's that of a bonfire that has burnt down from its original intensity and where the burning sticks have been scattered on the ground, charred black in places, still glowing red in places with a few small flames licking around them. I believe this is a picture both of the Church – where the sticks are individual congregations – and of churches, where the sticks are individual believers. For centuries the devil has been poking and scattering, isolating people, isolating congregations, always working to destroy unity and weaken the Church. I believe that God is gathering those burning pieces of wood together. He is leaning over them, His heart bursting with love, the marriage of the Lamb bright in His vision, blowing, blowing, blowing. As He rearranges those embers and burning brands new relationships will be formed and old structures broken. To be an army of Gideons in these last days we need to let Him gather us where the flames are and let His *agape* fill our lives: then we can set our world on fire.

Bible references

Isaiah 40:15
1 Corinthians 13:9
Matthew 9:27-31
Acts 10: 38
Luke 4:18
Isaiah 61:1
1 Peter 1:16
Ephesians 4:30
2 Corinthians 4:7
John 15:16
Galatians 5:6
1 Corinthians 13:2
1 Peter 1:22
Matthew 11:5

James 5:16
Song of Songs 8:6, 13-14
Revelation 22:17
Matthew 25:1-13
Revelation 1:20 John 17:26
Ephesians 3:14-21
John 14:23

Bookshelf

Here are a few of the books that I have found helpful, or simply inspiring, over the years. Some are referred to in these pages; others aren't.

Andrew Baker
Heavenly Visions

Heidi Baker
Compelled by Love

Mike Bickle
Passion for Jesus
Growing in the Prophetic

Shawn Bolz
Translating God
The Throne Room Company

Tim Cameron
The Forty-Day Word Fast

Mahesh Chavda
Only Love Makes a Miracle
Storm Warrior

David Yonggi Cho
The Fourth Dimension

Graham Cooke
Developing Your Prophetic Gifting
A Divine Confrontation

Jack Hayford
Rebuilding the Real You

Timothy Heller
Counterfeit Gods

Benny Hinn
Good Morning Holy Spirit

Rick Joyner
The Harvest

Daniel Kahnemann
Thinking, Fast and Slow

Kathryn Kuhlman
Nothing is Impossible with God

John Ortberg
If You Want to Walk on Water You've Got to Get Out of the Boat

Derek Prince
Blessing or Curse – You Can Choose

P.S. Rambabu
Dare to Win

Edith Schaeffer
L'Abri

Terry Virgo
No Well-worn Paths

Colin Urquart
Anything You Ask

Smith Wigglesworth
On Spiritual Gifts
Smith Wigglesworth: The Complete Collection of His Life Teaching (ed. Roberts Liardon)

ABOUT THE AUTHOR

Bob Hext is married to Anne. They have three daughters, Shelley, Elizabeth and Ionë, and (at the time of writing) four grandchildren. Bob leads the prophetic ministry at Wildwood Church, a Christ Central (New Frontiers) church in Stafford UK., where he is on the preaching and worship teams. He used to be an English teacher, and now runs a business with Anne supplying educational resources for children with dyslexia. He enjoys wildlife, taking photographs, and just being outside in the beauty of God's creation – preferably in the sunshine.